ADDRESSES

CELEBRATING THE CENTENNIAL

OF

RELIGIOUS JOURNALISM

A Retrospective of the work of Elias Smith, The Herald of Gospel Liberty, and those he inspired, 1809-1908

Edited by

REV. J. PRESSLEY BARRETT, D.D.

Editor *Herald of Gospel Liberty*

Charleston, AR
COBB PUBLISHING
2022

Published in the United States of America by:
Cobb Publishing
704 E. Main St.
Charleston, AR 72933
CobbPublishing.com
Editor@CobbPublishing.com
479.747.8372

ISBN: 979-8-3303-2316-6

I do in the first place publicly declare, that the Holy Scriptures which contain a revelation of the will of God, are the only sure, authentic and infallible Rule of the faith and practice of every Christian, by which all opinions are to be fairly and impartially examined; and in consequence of this, I protest against setting up and allowing the decrees of any man, or body of men, as of equal authority and obligation with the word of God; whether they be councils, synods, convocations, associations, missionary societies, or general assemblies; whether ancient or modern, Romish, Episcopal, Presbyterian, Congregational, Baptist, or Methodist, Popes, Fathers, or Doctors of Divinity.
—Elias Smith.

ELIAS SMITH
(Born June 17, 1769. Died June 29, 1846)
The FOUNDER OF RELIGIOUS JOURNALISM

First page of the first issue of the first religious newspaper.

HERALD OF GOSPEL LIBERTY.

BY ELIAS SMITH.

No. 1.]　　THURSDAY EVENING, SEPTEMBER 1, 1808.　　[VOL. 1.

"FROM REALMS FAR DISTANT, AND FROM CLIMES UNKNOWN, WE MAKE THE KNOWLEDGE OF OUR KIND YOUR OWN."

ADDRESS TO THE PUBLIC.

To the subscribers for this paper, and to all who may hereafter read its contents.

FRIENDS AND FELLOW CITIZENS,

THE age in which we live, may eventually be distinguished from others in the history of Man, and particularly, as it respects the people of these United States, the increase of knowledge is very great in different parts of the world, and of course there is an increase of *Liberty* among the people, and an increasing disposition in certain individuals, accompanied with their trontlous exertions, to prevent them from enjoying what they have been taught belongs to them, as a right given by their Creator, and guaranteed by the government of the country in which we live.

The struggle which has and still continues to convulse the nations in the old countries, are in a great measure over here. *Liberty* as men, is what many are now making violent exertions to obtain, and others (though few in number) by every possible mean are endeavouring to prevent.

This Liberty which first attracted attention in this country, to the great advantage of Millions and the grief of thousands, "who care not for the people;" but while we glory in being a free people, and of being independent of the nations which endeavoured to deprive us of the rights which God has given us in common with all nations, multitudes are enslaved with the principles brought from Europe by those who first settled this country. Had George the third, when he withdrew his troops from this country, withdrawn all the principles respecting civil and religious affairs, which are in opposition to the rights of mankind, we should have been a much more united and happy people than we now are; but alas! they are left among us like the Canaanites in ancient times, to be overcome by little and little; and like the army of God, which fell upon the mountains of Israel they are to be buried by men employed for that purpose, while every passenger is to erect a monument, whenever he finds a bone in his way. It is not now a tyrannical government which deprives us of liberty; but the highly destructive, principles of tyranny which remain in a good government; and though these principles are not protected by law, yet men's attachment to them, in a free government, prevents the enjoyment of Liberty which God has given us, and which all might enjoy according to the Constitution of the United States. A member of Congress said to me not long ago (while speaking upon the state of the people in this country, as it respects Religious Liberty) to this amount, "the people in this country are in general freer, as to political matters; but in things of religion, multitudes of them are apparently ignorant of what Liberty is." This is true, many who appear to know what belongs to them as citizens, and who will contend for their rights; when they talk or act upon things of the highest importance, appear to be guided wholly by the opinions of designing men, who would bind them in the chains of ignorance all their days, and entail the same on all their posterity. The design of this paper is to shew the *liberty* which belongs to men, as it respects their duty to God, and each other.

It is an established principle with me, that the man who appears in any public service and is faithful to his trust, will have a double character; by the unjust and them who judge from the testimony of such, he will be considered a disturber of the peace, as turning the world upside down, and stirring up the people to revolt; but by the well informed lovers of truth, he will be considered a light to them who otherwise would sit in darkness. There is no doubt in my mind but many will be displeased at what may appear in this paper from time to time, unless they own that, *right is equal among all.*

How difficult the task may be, which is now undertaken, is unknown to me, experience will shew this;—this however is my design, to have a steady and persevering regard to truth, and the general good of men; and to treat every thing in a fair and manly way; not scandalizing any, or doing any thing by partiality. Should any scandalize themselves by bad conduct; let them not charge it to me. If men do not wish to have bad things said of them, let them not do bad things. It is my design in the following numbers to give a plain description of the rights of men, and to shew the principles on which they are founded, and likewise to shew the opposite. There are many things taking place in the present day respecting religion, which will be noticed as they occur. A particular attention will be paid to the accounts of revivals of religion in different parts of the world, among the various denominations who call Jesus Lord, so far as it can be obtained.

A religious Newspaper, is almost a new thing under the sun; I know not but this is the first ever published to the world.

The utility of such a paper has been suggested to me, from the great use other papers are to the community at large. In this way almost the whole state of the world is presented to us at once. In a short and cheap way, a general knowledge of our affairs is diffused through the whole; and by looking into a Newspaper, we often look at the state of nations, and see them rise into importance, or crumble into ruin. If we see profited in political affairs in this way, I do not see why the knowledge of the Redeemer's kingdom may not be promoted or increased in the same way. It appears to me best to make the trial. The liberal subscriptions for this work in these trying times, have encouraged me to begin it, hoping that others will find an advantage in forwarding this work by adding their names to the list of those who have already wished such a work to appear in the world.

There are many things which will be taken up which are not new, but are important, and which, if stated to the rising generation will serve to give them a knowledge of that liberty for which their fathers bled, and for which they ought to contend.

It is the design of the Editor, in describing the nature of civil and religious *Liberty*, to come to the capacities of those whose advantages have been small, as to acquiring a general knowledge of the world.

It may be that some may wish to know why this paper should be named the "Herald of Gospel Liberty." This kind of Liberty is the only one which can make us happy, being the glorious Liberty of the sons of God which Christ proclaimed; and which all who have, are exhorted to stand fast in, being that which is given and enjoyed by the law of Liberty; which is the law of the spirit of life in Christ Jesus, which makes free from the law of sin and death.

In this place, I give the meaning of the word *Herald.* This word is derived from the Saxon word *Hereheald,* and by abbreviation, *Herald,* which in that language signifies the Champion of an army, and growing to be a name of office, it was given to him who, in the army, had the special charge to denounce war, to challenge to battle and combat, to proclaim peace, and to execute martial messages. The business of an Herald in the English government is as follows:—" To marshal, order, and conduct all royal ceremonies, to proclaim royal marriages, installations, creations of Dukes, Marquises, Earls, Viscounts,

THE TREE OF RELIGIOUS JOURNALISM

CONTENTS

In Meeting—

We introduce our friends by name. So, permit me to present to you A Centennial of Religious Journalism. The name is a sufficient introduction, since the book tells the story of the beginning, growth and influence of "Religious Journalism," as it has wrought so mightily to give to the Twentieth Century the best Christian civilization the world has ever seen, and to the church the best equipment for service it has had in its history as a means of reaching and teaching the people. Another has said that the "Religious Newspaper" is the university for the people.

Elias Smith, the founder of the first religious newspaper, was a prophet, and more than a prophet, for he planned for things he had not yet seen, and accomplished a greater work than ever he dreamed of—and he richly deserves a place of love and honor in the hearts of all Christians, and—a monument in some enduring form that shall perpetuate to coming generations a proper estimate of his worth to the church and to the world, emphasizing the nobility of his character, the strength of his wisdom, the courage of his heart, the faith of his life and the fruitfulness of his labors among and for men.

September 15-17, 1908, representative men from various denominations assembled in the city of Portsmouth, N.H., down by the sea, where one hundred years before, Elias Smith began religious journalism in the publication of the "Herald of Gospel Liberty."

The addresses delivered on that occasion are herein given to the public as in some measure indicating the appreciation of the life and labors of Elias Smith as a prophet and a reformer. But this book will best tell its own story in its own way, and to this end we leave it and the reader together.

Dayton, Ohio, December 25, 1908.

PORTSMOUTH AND THE CENTENNIAL
BY REV. A.H. MORRILL, D.D.

Of course, the most fitting place in which to celebrate the CENTENNIAL OF RELIGIOUS JOURNALISM was that where the paper had its beginning, the old city of Portsmouth. N.H.

Not only is Portsmouth the only seaport along the eighteen miles of the New Hampshire coast, but it is one of the oldest towns in New England, and hence is rich in historic events.

It is claimed that Captain Martin Pring, a skillful navigator of Bristol, England, under commission of the merchants of that city, came to the New World, and was the actual discoverer of New Hampshire, entering the harbor of Portsmouth some seventeen years before the landing of the Pilgrims at Plymouth, Mass.

In 1614, the celebrated Captain John Smith, the founder of Virginia, came to Portsmouth and praised the river at this point because of its depth, which at low tide is not less than forty-five feet, making it one of the finest harbors on the Atlantic coast.

The regular settlement of Portsmouth was made in 1623, though that portion where permanent dwellings were erected is now within the bounds of the present town of Rye. In 1631, the "Great House," so called, was built at the corner of Court and Water Streets, and from that time on the town has been growing until it covers its present area. In its earlier days, the settlement was known as "Strawberry Bank," because many strawberries grew upon what was known as Church Hill, but in 1653, in response to a petition made by the inhabitants, the name was changed to Portsmouth.

While a century seems a long time to most of us, and while the last century has been one in which remarkable progress has been made, yet the town where the first established religious paper celebrated its one hundred years of life had a history reaching back nearly one hundred and ninety years, with at least two church organizations having a history of two hundred and seventy years, the Congregational and St. John's Protestant Episcopal churches, while another has a history of about two hundred years. Besides these three churches, the Christian church is antedated by only the Universalist church, the other seven churches being of more recent establishment than the Christian.

It is eminently appropriate that the Centennial. Exercises should be held in other churches as well as in the Christian church. It was a celebration of RELIGIOUS JOURNALISM. as well as the centennial of the *Herald of Gospel Liberty*. The Congregational, Unitarian and Universalist church organizations are all older than the *Herald*, though their houses of worship are each less than a century old, while the Methodist church, in which one service was also held, was erected in 1827, yet the church was organized in 1808, and is thus of the same age as the *Herald*.

Among the places of historic interest visited by many of those attending the Centennial, was old St. John's church, where the "Vinegar Bible"[1] was seen, as well as Memorial Tablets, the pew occupied by Daniel Webster, the bell that was captured from the French at Louisburg, and once recast by Paul Revere, and once since, now used to summon the worshipers to the services of this ancient church, and other objects of interest.

Some of the delegates saw the first pipe organ brought to America, now in the chapel of St. John's church. It was brought from England in 1709 or 1710, and was set up first in a private house in Cambridge, Mass., later in King's Chapel, Boston, then in St. Paul's church, Newburyport, and in 1836 it was bought for $450, and brought to this chapel where it has since remained.

Another place of interest, and more than a century old is the Portsmouth Navy Yard, located on an island which is a part of the town of Kittery, Maine, which many visited at the close of the celebration, having opportunity to view the room where the treaty between Japan and RUSSIA WAS signed, as well as enjoying the privileges of going aboard a war vessel that was anchored at the yard.

It was also a matter of interest that the first religion newspaper in the United States was printed upon the saint press on which the first paper in New Hampshire. *The New Hampshire Gazette*, was printed, and also to know that that paper, begun October 7, 1756, has been published continuously until the present day. That press was exhibited at the World's Fair in Chicago, 1893, and is owned

---

[1] Called the "Vinegar Bible" because in one passage the word *vineyard* was spelled vinegar.—Editor.

now by a printing press company in New York City.

Another religious enterprise, in which almost all Christians at the present time take great Interest, the Sunday- school, found hearty supporters in Portsmouth in its infancy. In 1803, Mrs. Amos Tappan, the sister of the pastor of the North Congregational church, gathered the negro children at her house on Sundays and gave them religious instruction, while that church established a Sunday-school in its vestry in 1818, which was removed to Jefferson Hall after a little time, where children of all denominations received instruction.

The city itself, with its stately old business blocks, several more than a century old, its many mansions built before the birth of the *Herald*, yet well preserved, as well as its many modern buildings and homes, its beautiful school buildings and inviting churches, its swiftly flowing river and nicely shaded streets, its invigorating atmosphere laden with the odor of the ocean but three miles away, the cordial welcome and brotherly fellowship of the pastors and churches of the various denominations, all conspired to make the two or three days sojourn of the delegates and visitors of great delight, adding much to the interest of the important anniversary that was the reason for the gathering.

Whatever was the spirit of the people of Portsmouth a hundred years ago, whatever of sectarian rivalry or denominational intolerance might have prevailed, certainly during the three days of the Centennial there was an exemplification of the one hundred and thirty-third Psalm and the evidence that the Savior's prayer in the seventeenth chapter of John was answered in a large degree, so far as the Christians of Portsmouth, and those visiting the city, were concerned.

No less than ten different denominations were represented by their presence or participation in the meeting. But the unity of the Spirit and the bond of peaceful and delightful fellowship were constantly in evidence.

When the 200th anniversary of *Religious Journalism* is celebrated, at which none of us, who were privileged to attend the recent Centennial, will be present, except in spirit, if the advancement in the line of true progress shall be as great as that of the past hundred years, the millennium must be near at hand, and the world must be very nearly under the complete dominion of the King of kings.

COURT STREET CHRISTIAN CHURCH
Headquarters of the Centennial Celebration

5

WELCOME FROM THE COURT STREET CHRISTIAN CHURCH
BY REV. F.H. GARDNER, Pastor

Mr. President and Delegates to the Centennial of Religious Journalism: —

I am reminded tonight of a picture which appeared on the front cover of *The Endeavor World,* some two or three years ago.

The father and mother had begun the Thanksgiving dinner alone, but in the midst of it, the stage drove up and when the mother arrived at the window, she saw her boy coming toward the door. The feeling of glad delight written on the faces of the old  people; I shall never forget. Glad as was the young man, happier far were they who welcomed him home.

In one of my parishes, I had a very fine, elderly woman, whose boys were away from home the greater part of the time. They always seemed to enjoy a visit to the village, but it meant vastly more to that mother, shut out from the world at large, to have her sons come home to her.

So, after a century of time, you have come back home; to the first home of the *Herald of Gospel Liberty*, the birthplace of Religious Journalism. As much as this may mean to you, I am quite sure that it means much more to us.

There is something about one's birthplace that seems almost like sacred ground. One of my teachers, speaking of the home of his childhood said to me: "Yes, I have sold the farm, but I have reserved the right to roam over the lots, to peek into the barn, and to pick up some apples in the orchard. I couldn't give it all up."

So, tonight as you gather here to celebrate this anniversary, we welcome you back to the sacred spot of the birthplace of Religious Journalism.

I am reminded in your gathering here that we are not to despise the day of small things. It was only a switch, turned by a young woman which caused the fifty tons of dynamite to explode in the blasting of Henderson's Point, just below our city. The key pin in machinery is a very small piece of iron, but a most essential part in the operating of the same.

I do not believe for a moment that there would be many pulpits open to Elder Elias Smith, if he were among us now as he was a century ago, but in the sending forth of that little four-page *Herald* from his home on Jeffrey Street he set in motion an influence which today touches every race on the face of the whole earth.

In many ways religious journalism is a greater power for the kingdom of God than is the pulpit itself. I am not ashamed of our *Herald* of today, but let me call it simply the match which has started all this fire of religious journalism and who is there of us that would not feel justly proud to be the promoter of that match?

I am reminded, too, of the humble beginnings of other great and potent agencies, which are at work for the uplift of mankind. The kneeling of those college boys around the hay-stack as the beginning of modern missions; the gathering of those few boys by George Williams in that upper room as the beginning of the Y.M.C.A., with its magnificent buildings and its work among men of all classes; the assembling of those street boys in Sooty Alley by Robert Raikes as the starting of our great Sunday-school movement.

I believe this city ought to feel a just pride in giving birth to a movement whose hundredth anniversary we are about to celebrate. I can say as pastor of this church, I rejoice that we can boast that it was the founder of this church who first gave to the world a religious newspaper.

In nearly every town or city one will find some historic place which is almost sacredly guarded by the residents of that section. More than likely, it may not have much bearing on the world outside, but to those whose ancestors had a part in its history, it means very much. I do not know that the sermons of Elder Elias Smith have much bearing on the world of today. One thing is evident, that the outgrowth of Christian fellowship and the desire to spread the news of God's kingdom on earth, two important things for which he contended, are everywhere manifested.

In closing, I would say that we are here tonight fulfilling prophecy. It is not well for me to open the full history of the ministerial life of a century ago. Could they be here tonight, they would be the happiest of us all. History may portray that they had conflicts, and quarrels, and no use for each other, but I think it was more of a case of a misunderstanding. A century has had to elapse to bring around their hopes; and this gathering of these days in the different churches of our city is the fulfillment for which they all contested.

I have felt somewhat out of place in extending these words of greeting at this time. It has seemed to me, that one whose ministry goes back to the earlier days of our church life, who was pastor of this church in the close of the sixties and the opening of the seventies, and who still worships with us might better have been chosen. I refer to the Rev. C.P. Smith. Or one whose pastorate was the longest since that of Elder Smith, Rev. John A. Goss. Or better still, he who did so much to the upbuilding of the church, and the oldest living ex-pastor, Rev. Thomas Holmes.

However, in the name of the entertaining churches of Rye, Kittery and Portsmouth, in behalf of a long line of godly men who have served this church as pastors, I bid you welcome to the old home of the *Herald of Gospel Liberty*, the scene of the birthplace of Religious Journalism.

WELCOME FROM THE CITY
BY HON. WALLACE HACKETT, Mayor

I am happy to extend to you the greetings of the City of Portsmouth and a cordial welcome. We are glad to have you come to our old and historic city to hold your celebration. It is most fitting and appropriate to do so.

Portsmouth has been singularly fortunate in its association with certain great moral and historical events. This centennial observance of yours is not the least among them. I will not enlarge upon this event, as it is more fully within your knowledge than my own. But I will call your attention briefly to one or two occurrences of a similar nature which make good my claim that this locality is entitled to your veneration as the home and the starting place of certain influences which have grown as the country has grown, until now the modest days of their beginning are treasured among the valued memories of the past.

Here one of the earliest newspapers published in this country was established. It is still published here and has now the honor of being the oldest publication with a continuous and unbroken existence in the United States. *The New Hampshire Gazette,* established October 7, 1756, by Daniel Fowle, still appears weekly, as it has for more than a hundred and fifty years.

In October, 1856, the centennial anniversary of the introduction of printing in New Hampshire was celebrated in this city. It was a celebration worthy of the cause. A general holiday was observed. The town was decorated; a large military and civil procession occurred; an orator of the day. a banquet, and speeches and letters from distinguished individuals followed in due course; all indicating the importance of the event in the minds of the people of that time.

The Portsmouth Journal, 1793, published here until quite recently, originally under the name of the *"Oracle of the Day"* enjoyed, aside from its able publishers, the editorship of some of our most eminent citizens.

Daniel Webster commenced in its columns his career as a political writer. Levi Woodbury, Governor, United States Senator, and

Judge of the Supreme Court of the United States, was a frequent contributor.

Probably the earliest religious magazine published in America had its home here. The "Piscataqua Evangelical Magazine" began publication in 1805, but not possessing the strength and virility of the *Herald of Gospel Liberty*, it did not long endure. It is a very rare thing for any magazine, especially one devoted to a particular line of thought and development, to have as long and honorable career as that of the publication whose centennial is about to be observed.

Among the literary celebrities in the early days of this city was the gifted and profligate Joseph Bartlett, whose poems and aphorisms were celebrated in their day. At the funeral of John Hale, he recited a poem containing this epigram:

> *God takes the good*
> *Too good by far to stay;*
> *And leaves the bad,*
> *Too bad to take away.*

It was in these surroundings and in a company of men, who were giants in their day, that Elias Smith felt the call to publish his *Herald of Gospel Liberty*. That it has continued a hundred years diffusing hope, comfort and inspiration in countless households and among myriads of Individuals, is a subject of great congratulation and pride. His work has passed on to your able hands. You should realize, as I have no doubt you do, that you are trustees for posterity, and pass the trust along to your successors in undiminished strength and usefulness.

In conclusion I want to say that the City of Portsmouth feels honored by your presence here on this occasion. We trust its purposes may be most successful and gratifying; that you will enjoy your short stay with us; and I particularly commend to your attention the many historical places of interest which are easily accessible.

WELCOME FROM NEW ENGLAND
BY REV. A.H. MORRILL, D.D.,
President of the New England Christian Convention

MR. PRESIDENT AND FRIENDS:—You have already listened to words of greeting and welcome from the pastor of this church, from the president of the local Ministers' Association and from His Honor, the Mayor, and surely you and those with you who have come a full day's journey to the birthplace of Religious Journalism, properly to celebrate this Centennial, an event of far-reaching importance, must begin *to* feel at home in Yankee land. But that

REV. A. H. MORRILL, D. D.

you may be relieved of the last remnant of doubt, I am to speak a word of welcome for all the people of New England who acknowledge as their denominational name the simple title of Christian.

Be assured, then, in their behalf, that you are several thousand times welcome within our borders, to this historic seaport of the "Old Granite State," to this birthplace of the first religious journal in the new world. We welcome you because we are glad to fellowship the members of our denominational family.

As you have fostered and sustained the *Herald* or GOSPEL LIBERTY for the last forty years, we are glad to welcome your visit to the old home, as the people of this state welcome the return of their sons and daughters during "Old Home Week."

Little did Elias Smith forecast the future when he sent forth that first copy of the *Herald of Gospel Liberty*, September 1, 1808, a diminutive sheet of only four pages, that one hundred years later the centennial of that paper would be celebrated in the city of its birth, the scene of his labor for several years, attended with depri-

11

vation, trials and sacrifice. Little did he think that the child of his tears, prayers and labors, grown in one hundred years to a stalwart thirty-two-page paper, would become one of a company of able journals whose mission is the advocacy of the gospel, the heralding of glad tidings, telling of the work of millions of Christians, among whom there is the splendid spirit of Christian fraternity, which causes us almost to forget that any of the great family of Christians are of any other than our own fold. Little did he think that such a celebration as this would take place, and that the doors of the Methodist, Congregational, Unitarian and Universalist churches, as well as our own, would be open for these services.

How great results have been achieved from how small and humble beginnings! Then, Mr. President, I would have you and your associates assured that your New England welcome is from all Christian people, and all those who are friends of the cause of Christ and Christian work. While I have no official relationship to all the churches of New England, I think I know enough of the spirit of Christians of every name in this section to assure you that the welcome I am privileged officially to give you is truly representative of the Christian greeting which the one great family, including all the folds, would give you if the opportunity were theirs.

Such a celebration as this could not have occurred one hundred years ago! Think of it! Our program has on its representatives of several denominations, while yet others are deeply Interested in this celebration.

The world is being bound more closely together. Material advancement is overcoming petty jealousies and national hostilities. Educational institutions are doing much to realize the brotherhood of nations. The gospel seeks to bring all men into the realization of universal oneness and sympathy, because we are all the children of God, and are to live together as brethren and sisters of God's family. The burden of bringing the blessed gospel to the acceptance of every nation, class, rank, condition of humanity, rests upon all Christians.

The gigantic work of overcoming and destroying sin and injustice, of removing temptation, of creating heavenly conditions here, that men may prepare for heaven hereafter, is a compelling force that helps to solidify the ranks of Christian workers while, as the true spirit of the gospel becomes more fully appreciated, its devotees realize more and more the duty and privilege of Christian co-operation and fellowship.

I am glad to bear testimony to the larger, richer, fuller fellowship among Christians today in our New England.

Denominational organizations are not in hostile array against each other; Christian tolerance is growing into Christian fraternity and love.

Could Elias Smith and Abner Jones, to name only these two of the early fathers of our denomination in this section, return to us today and witness the spirit of Christian unity and fellowship in the very fields where they labored, methinks they would rejoice to see their desires so fully met among all Christians, and would feel like saying: "Now let Thy servants depart in peace, for our eyes have seen Thy salvation."

I am glad beyond any words I can use, to welcome you to our beloved New England; yes, to my own native state, that you may "behold how good and pleasant it is for brethren to dwell together in unity," though belonging to different ecclesiastical organizations, yet having the earnest of the Spirit and seeking rather to save men and thus advance the kingdom of God, than to build up sect or denomination.

Shall we not all pray that this commemoration may be potential in strengthening the bonds of Christian fellowship in the ranks of the religious press, and in all the commonwealth of Christians?

RESPONSE TO THE ADDRESSES OF WELCOME

BY JUDGE O.W. WHITELOCK,
President of the Christian Publishing Association

It is with pleasure that, on behalf of the Christian Publishing Association, the delegates representing the Christian conferences of the United States and Canada, and on behalf of the invited representatives of other churches and religious publications here assembled, I am privileged to respond to these words of welcome, coming as they do from the pastor of the Christian church of this

city, from the president of her Ministerial Association, from the Mayor, the executive officer of one of the oldest New England towns and chief port of the State of New Hampshire, and from the president of the New England Convention. We appreciate the kind words you have expressed and the hand of fraternal greetings extended to us all.

The Christian church of this city, and whose especial guests we are, is one of the oldest of the Christian churches, having been organized by Rev. Elias Smith, January 1, 1803, over one hundred years ago. He was pastor of this church when he published the first religious newspaper, the *Herald of Gospel Liberty*, on the 1st day of September, 1808. It is in honor of this event in the world's history and development that we are congregated in this historic spot to celebrate its centennial anniversary.

All great events have their inception somewhere and at some time, but the initial step or the inceptive hour is often difficult to fix. The silent forces which produce a given result, many times cannot be traced with precision from their Inception. Sometimes an important event or a great idea is centuries developing and when it finally bursts upon the world as an active force, the one who brings it to the world's attention and who gets the honor for the discovery or the invention is often not the one that had the conception or first saw the vision. The one who brings the fruition is the one, however, whom the world delights to honor. The idea of a religious newspaper was not original with Elias Smith, as he himself testifies, but he caught the vision of its Importance and had the courage to put the idea into motion and make it a tangible entity and reality as a medium to disseminate religious facts and happenings and a vehicle to convey the ideas of a dawning religious liberty. Elias Smith had ideas that be believed the world ought to know. This was the important incentive which led to the publication of the *Herald of Gospel Liberty*, one hundred years ago. These Ideas were as a flame of fire in the mind and heart of Smith. These ideas were the result of hundreds of years of development on the one hand, and yet were the outgrowth of hundreds of years of tyranny on the other. Liberty was the burning, throbbing thought in the mind of Smith. Religious liberty was the vision he saw, new, yet old. The seed thought was planted by the Prince of Peace, the man of Galilee, and was brought to fruitage in the time of the apostles and early Christians to be shackled by the mailed hand of the tyrant and strangled to the death gurgle by the bloody hand of a Nero. In the Dark Ages the lamp of liberty had gone out and the world writhed and groaned beneath the hand of the oppressor. Liberty was throttled and chained, her flickering light had gone out in the darkness and gloom that overspread the world. But the time came when the clanking chains of the oppressor began to loosen, and the pine knot and tallow dip of liberty began to dispel the darkness of tyranny, as the feudal barons forced king John at Runnymede to grant the Magna Charta.

That immortal document brought the dawn of civil liberty and gave a glimpse of the true Inheritance of man which was his first estate. The unwritten law of England was the development of certain inalienable rights. The Puritan Fathers touched New England's shores and made Plymouth Rock a sacred spot. They brought to America the seeds of political and religious freedom; these were planted in the virgin soil of the New World.

The candle had been set upon a candlestick; its dim light lit up New England's rock-bound coast and kindled the fire whose flames began to burn up the venom of tyranny as the hydra head of the monster crossed the ocean waves and fastened its tentacles upon the promised land of liberty, the Canaan which was to flow with the milk and honey that would nourish the world.

From the candle of Plymouth Rock was lighted the torch of liberty that burst forth at Boston, Concord, Lexington and Bunker Hill, that touched the fuse that fired the shot of liberty heard "around the world." Faneuil Hall was ablaze; sparks from burning Charlestown fell like star showers upon the Green mountains, the flames crept up to their summits and cast gleams of light upon the white capped peaks of New Hampshire. The fires of liberty had begun to burn not only on New England hills and the plains of Boston, but in the plantations of Virginia, the pine-clad hills of the Carolinas, among the Dutch of New York and the Quakers of Pennsylvania. Its cloven tongues of fire fell upon Patrick Henry, touched the pen of Jefferson and set a diadem in the hilt of the unsheathed sword of Washington.

The fires of civil liberty burned in city, village and country. The fires of patriotism filled true American hearts. The old Liberty Bell in Independence Hall, pealed forth to the world the glad notes of liberty from the oppressor's hand. The Declaration of Independence laid anew the foundation of civil liberty and blazed the way for a broader and deeper religious freedom.

In a humble home in Connccticut, June 17, 1769, was born Elias Smith. He breathed the atmosphere of freedom and was rocked in the cradle of religious fervor. The stirring times of the Revolution must have fired his young heart, for on the 6th anniversary of his birth the battle of Bunker Hill was fought. Is it any wonder that his soul was moved and his deep religious zeal aroused as he thought of the world and even his own native land being bound by a theology of creeds, man-made, and based upon men's versions of the Bible? the creed or discipline, varying according to the view-point of their authors. A devout Baptist, Smith in 1792 was ordained an evangelist in the Baptist church, but his religious zeal would not be hedged in by the prescribed rules of that organization. He demanded greater freedom of religious thought and speech. He wrote articles setting forth his views; he was persecuted, and like most reformers was characterized as a crank and was ostracized and persecuted by the sectarian churches.

To have a means of defending his principles and to propagate his ideas of religious liberty, he published the *Herald of Gospel Liberty*, the first religious newspaper in the world.

The conception of the idea of a religious newspaper was not his own, but was suggested by Hon. Isaac Wilbur, a congressman from Rhode Island. The congressman suggested that Smith publish the paper while friends would provide the means. But Smith wanted a free-lance, if anything. He feared if friends provided the means that they would want to control the utterances of the paper. He decided to publish the paper at his own expense. This decision was characteristic of the liberty-loving views of the man. In the first issue Smith laid the foundation stone upon which he proposed to erect the structure of religious journalism. He said:

> The design of this paper is to show the liberty which belongs to men, as it respects their duty to God and to each other.

A splendid corner-stone—a noble purpose revealed—a declaration of principles almost as far-reaching and important as those enunciated in the Magna Charta or the new American Charter, the Declaration of Independence. He was beginning a great work. He had seen a vision; the seeds of liberty propagated for hundreds of years had at last brought forth that which would in time become a tree, destined in the progress of time to produce the golden apples of the millennium. But not yet, no, not yet!

While the tree, one hundred years ago, began to blossom and bring forth fruit in its season, yet all the fruit has not been sweet and luscious; much of it has been bitter. Smith himself, ate of its bitter fruit, for he was persecuted almost beyond measure, but the tree had been planted by living waters.

The *Herald of Gospel Liberty* has continued from the day of its birth to scatter seeds of truth that have taken root in minds and hearts until the world has been brought nearer and nearer to the ideal of its founder. The liberty which belongs to men in their relation to their God and to each other has not been attained. Men have fallen far short indeed. But the progress in a century has been great. The fellowship of Christian character which has been told and re-told and which was echoed and re-echoed, through the columns of the *Herald of Gospel Liberty*, has, in a large measure, come to be the sentiment of the Christian world. The partition walls between the churches are crumbling down, sectarianism is fast passing away. Creeds are being re-written or allowed to pass into innocuous desuetude. The religious world is embracing a broader fellowship, men are being recognized more and more for what they are, rather than for what they believe or say they believe.

There is today a liberty of religious thought and sentiment not dreamed of one hundred years ago, and of that order which makes the world better. Religious newspapers have had a large part in the development of this religious liberty. While the *Herald of Gospel Liberty* was the first religious journal to be published, other publications were soon to be established and are represented in this celebration today. Each has contributed its share in bringing the world nearer the feet of the Master, who taught the Golden Rule, but which a selfish world is slow to adopt as its rule of life.

The *Herald of Gospel Liberty* was founded as the personal organ or mouthpiece of Elias Smith, but it soon came to be recognized as the exponent of the doctrines of the Christian Church, then in its infancy. It soon came to be a recognized organ of that church and, in later years, came to be the official organ of the church. To-day every church has its religious newspaper and organ to present its peculiar doctrines or beliefs to the world. It is now a mighty force in the Christian world. But this class of papers is not confined wholly to expounding the doctrines of certain ecclesiastical bodies. Some are given to general church and religious news, as the *Christian Herald,* others to some great branch of Christian activity, as the *Sunday-School Times,* which is published to benefit the Sunday-schools of all churches, and the *Christian Endeavor World,* which is the official organ of the Christian Endeavor societies of all churches. The Christian liberty advocated by Smith and taught by the Christian Church for over one hundred years is today the fundamental principle of the Christian Endeavor movement.

The vision that Smith saw has, in a measure, come to be a reality in the Twentieth Century. The cords of love and Christian liberty are binding together, as with a chain of gold, all nations, kindreds and tongues, until the whole earth has begun to realize something of that liberty which makes men free, yet binds them to God and to each other.

While the founding of a religious newspaper did not seem a great movement to the neighbors and associates of Elias Smith; nor is it probable that he could look down the corridors of time with prophetic eye and see that the tree he had planted had grown until its branches had extended into almost every corner of the earth, and its fruit was being gathered in every clime, by every church, by every Sunday-school, by every mission society, by every Christian Endeavor society, by every church congress, by every church federation; yet one hundred years has shown the fulfillment of such a prophecy. At the time of the planting of the seed which produced the tree, it seemed to be less than all the seeds the church of Jesus Christ had planted, but when it was grown up it shot forth great branches, so that, indeed, the fowls of heaven have lodged under the shadows of its branches.

Its leaves have been indeed for the healing of the nations; it has brought peace on earth and good-will to men.

This city is indeed an historic spot. The message sent out from its portals one hundred years ago, like the dove sent out by Noah, returned after many days, carrying the olive branch of peace. When the paw of the Russian bear was torn and bleeding; when the great Goliath had been smitten in the forehead by a pebble from the sling of David; then it was that our own President stretched forth his hands and the dove of peace nested here. This was one of the greatest triumphs of the ages and the name of Roosevelt will go down in history as a man of peace, though trained in war. Like Grant, the great American Captain, he said, "Let us have peace." This is sacred ground; we are glad to be welcomed here and will remove the sandals from our feet and tarry with you.

METHODIST EPISCOPAL CHURCH
Where Wednesday Forenoon Session was held.

THE RELIGIOUS PRESS. THE EXPONENT OF RELIGIOUS FREEDOM
BY REV. F.H. PETERS[1]

My main apology for my part in this meeting is that I have found it quite impossible to bring the multiplied bigness of the subject assigned me within so brief a space of time. Religious Freedom and the Religious Press are vital factors in the religious history of the past century or two, as well as the foundation stones of this celebration and of the movement that makes it possible. And I shall attempt no more than to mention two or three of its phases which to me seem most important.

To the true American citizen few words are sweeter than freedom. It expresses the essential idea of his life. To define it, one must recount the nation's life-story, from the landing of the forefathers on these rugged New England shores, to the present struggle for justice in our civil, industrial, and social life. So firmly is the idea woven into the fabric of our life that it becomes at once the reed *by* which we test the Americanism of conflicts, principles, and men. The whole superstructure of our national idea is founded on liberty, and every important event in its development, at the heart, has been a plea for the freedom of the individual in body, mind, and soul.

Nor is freedom in religion in any sense a secondary consideration. It is first and fundamental to all that is worth while. To eliminate it would be to contradict our traditions and history, and to do

[1] Delivered on Wednesday forenoon, September 16th, in the M.E. church. Mr. Peters is pastor of the Christian church at Coshocton, Ohio.

violence to the dominating spirit of certain old world events most closely allied with the spiritual life and progress of the world.

The New Testament, and particularly the Gospels, is devoted to the cause of freedom in religion. The Gospel of Christ gives stinging rebuke to the attempt to force the yoke in matters of faith and practice. The basis of discipleship in the days of Jesus' active life, was more a question of attitude than of creed. The simple invitation, — "follow me," seems to have been sufficient; and this did not require the formal swallowing of all sorts of theological monstrosities, but simply to enter with the whole of the life and strength, into sympathetic fellowship with Him and His work. The most men needed to know of God was suggested in the familiar term, Father; and the whole reach of human obligation and responsibility to God and to humanity, is met in loving God with all the heart, and our neighbor as ourselves. The lives of the first disciples must be stirred with the spirit and life of the great Teacher, and their activities so Christ-like, both in spirit and in actual accomplishment, that men beholding, should know they "had been with Jesus and learned of Him." But one scans the New Testament in vain for the slightest hint that Jesus gave encouragement to any sort of theological bondage, and is forced to conclude that in their individual faith, He meant His disciples to be fresh and free as a summer morn. The necessity He lays upon His followers is consecration rather than conformity, and the ultimate test is the service they render in behalf of the redemption of the world. At the last Great Day, I think the vital question will be, not *what we thought* about the various theological opinions, but *how we wrought* in the actual warfare of life. And I doubt not that *how we loved* will be much more important than *what we believed.* In any case, the individual conscience must *be inviolate, since* everyone must render to God the account for his own life, and himself reap what he has sown.

A noted preacher of sometime past put it thus:

> From the manner in which Christ and His apostles introduced and established the Gospel, we learn that they considered religion a subject on which all men ought to think for themselves; to employ their own minds, to inquire,

to deliberate, to fix a serious impartial attention. It was the wish and intention of the great founder of our religion that His religion should be received on very different grounds from false religions, should have no support but what it derived from its own excellence. Christianity everywhere considers it a settled, conceded point, that men on the subject of religion are to exercise their own judgment and follow their own conviction.

Besides, we do not forget the books of the Bible are personal, and their visions and revelations are not to the state, nor to associations of men. They are to the individual life, —the seat of all permanent progress in righteousness, and from the human standpoint, the bulwark of the kingdom of God. The richest and finest sentiments of the Old Testament are statements of individual experiences, of blessings accruing to the single life, and of its boundless prospect for growth and glory. While many of Christ's most blessed words were addressed to certain misguided ones groping their way in sin, whose blinded eyes could not perceive the friendly light streaming out of the skies, and whose ears were deaf to the angelic voices announcing the presence of the kingdom of heaven and the world-wide hope of eternal life.

But apart from the teaching of the New Testament, freedom in religion has an important relation to character and to the growth of the spiritual life. This in my judgment is most vital indeed, a bedrock foundation on which we may safely rest the whole of our plea. Personal conviction is fundamental to all excellency. In the past it has made many lives worthy our great admiration, and given them prominent part in determining the course of world events. The striking thing in the lives of very many of the world's great ones, has been individual independence and conviction. And so far, as I know, none who have placed small value on their right to think for themselves, have had lasting influence in human affairs. The message of Jesus was independent of His time, and such as burned in His own soul. And behind the fruitfulness of the wonderful lives of Paul and others, were their conscientious conviction, untrammeled by authority of church, or the opinions of men. And since the world began, the highest personal character has been attained

24

by those who looked to personal freedom as a guiding star, and to whom individual rights in matters of faith and practice, were more than life.

The claim sometimes made, that the exercise of the right to think causes division, does not hold true. Certainly, divisions have come in this country of boasted religious liberty. But they are not due entirely to free investigation on the part of the people. In many cases they arise from the want of it. Ambitious men have taken advantage of the readiness with which the people receive whatever is heralded as truth, to proclaim their peculiar theories and to organize their sects, increasing confusion and retarding the cause they design to serve. I think Channing was right when he said:

> We must not imagine that the way to stifle sects is to encourage men to receive religious opinions without thought or inquiry. In a land of universal toleration, this is the most direct way of laying them open to imposition and enthusiasm. The only way to produce uniformity is to encourage serious and honest inquiry.

In the light of these considerations, very much of the actual doings of the religious world in its attitude toward freedom in religion, has been passing strange and much of it, directly counter to the spirit of the sacred books from which it professed to derive its authority, and to the common *rights* of man. We cannot forget, though the recollection causes us to shudder, that many of the fields through which the organized church has passed in its march up the centuries, are strewn with the bleaching bones of stifled convictions and murdered liberties; and that religious tyranny, self-appointed, bigoted and unashamed, arrayed in garments of pretended piety, and bearing aloft the sign of the cross, has dipped its feet in the blood of assassinated religious freedom and made its accursed and Indelible track across the face of the world.

But after all, have we not made great advancement toward better things, and are we not rejoicing that the old-time narrowness is passing away? Yes, we are rejoicing in this, and for every actual victory for our rights we should rejoice and be glad evermore. But what of the night? Is religious tyranny so completely routed from the field that it is no longer necessary to guard against its encroachments? Have we today, we of this great free country, and we of the Christians, of the broadest platform ever announced by a body of Christian believers, —have we the unchallenged right to private judgment in interpreting the Scriptures, and to follow conscience in questions of faith and practice? Hardly so, so long at least as there are whisperings that the attitude of a foremost American citizen toward a question of disputed theology should disqualify him for the highest office within the gift of the people. It seems to me the following, written some years ago by one of the keenest of men, is a fair statement of the present situation:

> We certainly have reason to thank God for the enjoyment of greater religious liberty than was ever possessed before. The fire of persecution is quenched; the Scriptures are in every man's hand. But still, to read the Scriptures with independent minds requires no little effort. There are still obstructions to the privilege of judging for ourselves. The spirit of popery did not expire among our ancestors with its forms. Human nature and its ruling passions are always the same. The same love of power, the same desire to lead, the same wish to dictate to the consciences of others, which burned in the breasts of the Romish clergy, and built up the Roman hierarchy, still subsist and operate among us. There is still and always will be, until man is more exalted by Christianity, a conspiracy against the religious and civil rights of men. In Protestant countries there are those who are impatient of contradiction, who wish to impose their views on others, who surround their creeds with similar terrors to those made use of by the Papal church, and doom to destruction all who have the temerity to differ from their opinions.

In a recent book, entitled "The Democracy of Religion," the author, one of our own men of large experience, says:

> Everybody believes that the Bible contains a revelation made to the individual, and not to any one man or set of men. Nobody believes that any one man, or set of men has

been divinely commissioned to Interpret the Bible for other people. Yet strange to say. If the individual to whom the revelation was made assumes the prerogative of reading and interpreting that revelation, he may learn by sad experience that he has entered upon a dangerous experiment. Nor will a beautiful life atone for his honest thinking, if perchance his opinions of Interpretations run counter to the opinions of those who ages ago assumed to fix metes and bounds to theological thinking.

But I think the better day is at hand. Surely within the last fifty years we have taken rapid strides toward the things that deserve to be. The persecutions of past centuries are no longer possible, and the leaven of our common rights bids fair to change the whole lump. The present is as much brighter than the time which some here can remember, as is the glorious morning brighter than the dark evening shadows. There is a better understanding and kindlier feeling among the various divisions of the Church of Christ, and the tendency everywhere is to recognize every one's right to inter-pret the Bible for himself, and to believe and worship according to the dictates of his conscience. And I think it will never again be possible for associated Christians to close the door of their fellow-ship to any who believe in Jesus and are willing to help spread the principles of His kingdom.

In the advocacy of these better things, several agencies have been active and influential.

The educational institutions of this country and of other coun-tries have borne a most noble part in the struggle for religious free-dom. They are still in the forefront, and to them, all who appreciate the right and privilege to think and to act, are under great and un-ceasing obligation. They have helped to send persecution out of Christian civilization, and to effectually bar its gates against its re-turn; and all the time they are determining factors in the world's life and progress by contributing to its working forces every year, scores of men and women whom no ignorance can discourage and no tyranny make afraid. And whenever I pass a seat of learning, whether university or country school, I feel like doffing my hat in recognition of its services to the cause of common freedom, *to* me, divine and sacred as life.

Then *the world has* received much and has much to expect from the spread of the republican idea in government Lincoln's comment on the slavery issue that "no government can long endure half slave and half free" fits the case exactly. Men who have civil liberty will not long wear the religious yoke. And if I mistake not. the insistent demand upon the part of the people in this country and in various other countries for their rights in the affairs of government, is a prophecy that the hour draws near when these same people will demand their God-given inalienable right to the unfettered exercise of freedom in religion.

The pulpit also has had a share in bringing the changes that have come. This share is important and beyond our power to estimate. But some of us feel that it has not been so great as it ought to have been. Candid survey of the past hundred years gives the impression that the clergy as a class, has not had the keenest appreciation of the absolute value of the exercise of personal freedom in religion in its relation to the culture of the best in human life. Doubtless very many have felt that the necessity to preach Jesus Christ as a personal Savior overshadowed everything else, and with deep concern for other things, lost sight of the cause of common rights. But this has not been true of all; for many of our country's greatest preachers, while pressing the claims of God on the individual life, failed not to raise their eloquent voices in opposition to religious bondage of every sort

Such pleas for truth by these brave men of God, continued in the face of opposition and threatened physical violence, could not fail of their effect. Naturally those who heard them gladly, organized that they might render effective assistance in its dissemination. And to a few such men with hearts aflame for the truth, and with voices which no theological decrees could hush, we are indebted for our life ns a distinctive people, and the proud distinction of having contended for these same blessed principles for more than a hundred years.

But of all the advocates of religious freedom, I think the religious press should have first place. Its position as an educational agency makes it possible for it to be the most powerful advocate.

The attitude of the public toward the press of the land is friendly and very much of what passes for public opinion, in its temper and spirit, is but the reflection of the temper and spirit of the public press. So true is this, that it is charged that the press, when it sets itself the task, is able to determine the course of events, to annul the force of the elective franchise in this free country, and to exert an influence in affairs second to no other agency. The readiness with which people accept what they read without serious question whether it be true, gives the press a leverage both peculiar and powerful.

Because of this it is of the most vital moment that the position of the press of the country on all matters involving the rights of the people, and pertaining to their life and progress, shall be exactly right. This is particularly true of the religious press. In its field, it is even more powerful; and with the added weight which the religious sentiment gives it in the average mind, what service in behalf of truth and righteousness is too great for it to render?

True, the usefulness of the religious press in favor of religious freedom has not, at all times, been equal to its opportunities; and no doubt a wide range of causes are involved in its failures.

Almost every religious publication has a constituency to represent. Ultimately of course, to serve the Kingdom of Righteousness, but as a means to that end, to defend and promulgate peculiarities of doctrine and of method pertaining to the people to whom it belongs. And so, it is no wonder if in the strife of creeds and methods of work, the attention of the religious press as a whole, has been directed to things other than religious freedom.

Besides, those responsible for the utterances of religious journals, (I refer to the editors) feeling the weight of possible influence and responsibility, have been cautious and conservative, preferring to err on the side of the old doctrines and ideas, than to so much as suggest that the truth may not lie there, lest the discovery cause some to fall. The result of this has been to cause some religious journals theoretically free, in their practical working, to become extremely unfree, and in the arena of actual conflict, unable to cast a shadow greater than the length and breadth of one man's mind. Am I right in concluding it were far better to follow the example of

Jesus and to speak the truth to the common people at whatever cost, trusting that God, whose own it is, will temper it as he tempers the wind, and by it make it make us free?

If I could have my way, every religious publication should set itself, unflinchingly, to bring the truth to light, even though some of that truth will neither wear the garments of past ages, nor ride in the livery of established theological opinions. And this I think would best be done by opening its pages to every man whose training and character give him the right to be heard. And it is my candid conviction that in doing so, the religious press of the country would pay its highest tribute to religious freedom, and render its greatest service to the truth of Almighty God.

Some religious journals were born free. They were conceived in liberty, and dedicated to the proposition "that in interpreting the Scriptures, all men are free and have equal rights." Among these is our own *Herald of Gospel Liberty*, the oldest in the world. And we of the Christians, to whom it belongs, have just pride that it is so. But of far greater consequence is the fact that it was born to make men free, and to herald the glad tidings of independent thinking and of gospel liberty. And it must be our constant concern to keep it true to its divine calling in its actual life as well as in its name. Of course, it must be faithful in directing attention to the kingdom of God in its world-wide aspect, and exhort to earnestness in the spiritual life; but it must also be the medium through which the best thought of our people shall find free expression, that by the candid and friendly interchange of ideas, we may come to the truth and preserve our liberties.

At the commencement of the second century of its life, we ought to dedicate it anew to the great principle of freedom in religious thought and faith; and our pledge must bind us to make it so in fact as well as in theory. Most certainly the latter will be the more difficult task, but our task it is, none the less, if we mean to be faithful to the principles we profess, and to the truth committed to our care.

We have been casting about for some worthy thing to undertake in this centennial year. It Is right that we should do so. It will be to our lasting shame if we do not attempt some work worthy of our talents and opportunities. I know not what the particular thing may be. But whatever else we conclude, let us resolve upon some more sublime devotion to the principles we have inscribed on our banner. If we can enter the new century of our life with some finer enthusiasm for the things in which we believe, our example will encourage others to join us, until our united strength shall force into dark oblivion the things that hinder the progress of righteousness. And finally, let us resolve that whatever "course others may take" our general church paper shall be so imbued with the spirit of our distinctive plea, that wherever it goes, it shall be the blessed harbinger of Gospel liberty, the steadfast exponent of religious freedom, and the constant and faithful witness for that Christ-like manhood and womanhood which is the basis of our Christian fellowship and the hope of the world.

> "In the beauty of the lilies, Christ was born across the sea, With a glory in His person, That transfigures you and me; As He died to make men holy, Let us live to make men free, While truth is marching on."

Coshocton, Ohio.

TYPE-METAL AT ITS BEST
BY S.D. GORDON[1]

The commonly accepted standard of value throughout most of the world today is gold. This centenary reminds us that there is a finer metal. Gold talks, but lead talks louder, whether in bullets or type-metal. The financiers usually decide whether a war shall be begun, but the soldiers decide how it shall be fought, and what the outcome shall be. Great wars have been conducted without much gold, but never without an abundance of lead.

And in type-metal the superiority is yet more marked. Gold talks, but lead talks more insistently, and is heard farther, and listened to more eagerly. Gold is worshiped, it's true; but brains is worshiped yet more by a large majority. Lead makes gold, brain creates money; type-metal controls the money markets.

There is a peculiar emphasis to type-metal. To the great crowd if a thing is in print, it's so. There is a mandate of authority about a printed statement. Even those who are somewhat initiated into the mysteries of bookmaking and paper-making do not wholly escape the influence of the peculiar emphasis of lead.

I write something down, but sometimes with a misgiving seizing me. The thing is true; but is it stated in the best way? And though true, is it the particular phase of truth that needs emphasis just now? An indefinable misgiving possesses me as I write it, due maybe largely to my physical or mental mood at the time. But, by and by, it comes back to me in proof-sheets, and as I read, I find myself saying, softly to myself, "Did I write that? It states the thing so clearly; it clearly is the thing

[1] Delivered on Wednesday morning, September 16th, in the M E. church. Mr. Gordon represented the *Sunday School Times,* Philadelphia, Pa.

to be said Just now, too." The type has given such an emphasis that my misgiving is overcome. The truth stands out with a daring boldness, a clear-cut positiveness because of its leaden medium of expression. Lead has great power of emphasis.

Papers have some great advantages over books in influencing men. Books are largely burial-places for Ideas, or sometimes simply for words in the absence of ideas. Few books live an active life. The vast majority are not read, or read partly, or read only once, and then shelved—burial-places of their contents. Some books exert a tremendous influence; but they are the few in comparison with the great mass printed.

The paper lacks the element of permanency that belongs to a book, but it has the great advantage of frequency. It has all the tremendous moral power of repetition; it comes again and again. There is an imperiousness about a paper coming in the mail to your home. It belongs to the group of imperious things for which you drop everything else for the moment. The telegram and telephone are imperious; you excuse yourself at once to answer their call.

There is the same kingly imperiousness about the printed paper. It comes at regular intervals in the mail, demanding to be taken up. It comes knocking insistently at your door, saying, "I'm the newest and latest and best thing. Drop those other things and listen to me." And it is surprising how largely its demand is granted.

The paper has the advantage of a larger audience than books. It has the same audience in the main, for book readers are paper readers, too. And then it has a far greater audience of those who are largely the non-book-reading sort. It is a different audience, too, in being less studious, and more impressionable. If a thing happens to strike right it is quite apt to influence the conduct. The impression may not go very deep, and again it may make radical changes. The book reader makes changes more slowly as a rule.

Type-metal has been a great factor in this remarkable century of progress. It has been a great unifier. Most wars have been due to strong prejudice; and that has been due to misunderstanding, and that to ignorance. Lead has been the great news exchange of the world. Through it has come better acquaintance, more knowledge, clearer understanding, kindlier feelings and a closer knitting up of race bonds. It has conducted a great university among the peoples of the earth in the science of free government, and in all that has made life so much better and higher and more intelligent than ever before.

But lead is at its best in giving the best Type-metal is at its highest and holiest service when used to tell men of Jesus. And religious journalism is concerned with bringing Jesus to men more practically and intimately and clearly. Jesus coming into a man's life gives him a new mental birth, as well as a new spirit birth. That is to say, He does if He is allowed full and free sway. That is a very big "if" needing the underscoring of several lines in blue pencil. When I try to read some books and some papers, I wish earnestly that there might have been a new mental birth for the writer. It would make much easier and better reading for me.

Religious journalism has the privilege of bringing to men that which affects all the crying questions of life. For Jesus changes everything He is allowed to touch with a free hand. He not only makes a man a new man, but a new husband, and father and home-maker; a new neighbor, and citizen, and customer, and voter.

If Jesus have sway in the life, a man becomes a more intelligent farmer, and mechanic, and tradesman, and financier, and statesman. The religious writer has the rare privilege of bringing to men a Jesus that affects every phase of life in the most radical way. But he himself needs the mental regeneration of a Jesus before he can use the type-metal at its highest.

There are some serious limitations in type. It is cold. It lacks the personality of the speaker. The warm presence. the sound of a human voice vibrant with life, the face, the eyes—it has to get along without these. That's a great limitation. Type of itself is cold. But it can be warmed, and that is the writer's great task, to transmit warmth to cold lead.

There are three ways of doing it. Type takes on the dominant mood of the man behind it. The man shoving the steel point can transmit through it to the type the fire of a dominant purpose. It is possible to put your heart into lead; though few do. But to do it the heart fires must be kept up.

You know that head and heart never drive A-team; they always go tandem, and usually with the head in the lead. But that's the wrong order; the heart should be in the lead. The brain may be as keen as the edge of a newly honed razor, and the walls of the intellectual storehouse bulging out with their wealth, and yet the heart hot and tender may be dominant over all. That is the first cure for the chill of type.

Then there can be the skillful use of coloring matter, to relieve the chill of plain black-and-white. The delicate use of color-words, adjectives and adverbs, just enough— not too much—it takes nice work—that gives the bit of glow to type that it needs.

But then there is the use of an after-fire. It is possible after the paper has gone out, a thousand miles away, to send after it a prayer that will make it glow into a new fire under the reader's eye. Prayer has more than subjective power. I don't need to be a Christian to believe that. I may be merely a student of occultism, of the philosophies of India, to believe in the objective power of prayer. But being a Christian with a Jesus and a Holy Spirit, I know with a new positiveness that by prayer L can send out an after-fire that shall set the printed page, a thousand miles away, all aglow and aflame as I pray.

The formula for making type-metal differs in different foundries, and is always interesting. A common formula is one hundred pounds of lead, forty of antimony, thirty of tin and sometimes six or seven of copper. Lead naturally is soft-hearted, and needs a bit of stiffening by its neighboring allies to be able to stand the pressure of active life. But I would urge upon religious journalists that having made up their type by whatever formula they may severally prefer, the metal should be given a bath, a sort of chemical bath to affect its quality. I would give it a bath of love.

And by love I don't mean the weak, wabbly, sentimental stuff that often uses that great word. Love itself is pure; it hates sin. It never compromises where sin is concerned. Love always carries a short-bladed, two-edged sword, with both edges whetted up to the finest pitch of sharpness, and never hesitates to use it against sin.

And love is loyal to its Chief. Love is divine; that is, it is of God.

"Strong Son of God; immortal love."

It must be loyal to its Chief—Jesus. Son of God, God the Son: Son of man, God a man! as human as though only human; as really God as though not a man. That is Love's Chief.

Yes, I would *go* yet farther. I would take the editor, who sends the current out through steel point to leaden types; I would make his brain as keen as razor's edge, his intellect as full as bulging storehouse, and then give him a bath, a habitual, continuous dousing and sousing in a bath of love. Then type-metal shall be at its best in giving the Best out to men.

RELIGIOUS JOURNALISM FOR YOUNG PEOPLE

BY AMOS R. WELLS[1]

I am especially glad to have part in this Centennial of Religious Journalism, for several reasons. In the first place, I have known and read the *Herald of Gospel Liberty* through practically all my life, and have watched with keen interest its steady progress. I have known most of its editors, and number them among my personal friends. I rejoice in the present success of this oldest of religious periodicals, which never has been so strong in every way as it is today. May we all grow old in the same glorious fashion!

In the second place, it is a pleasure to me to have a part in this celebration because of my long association with this body of Christians as a professor in Antioch College, which you founded. While there, and during my years in the service of the national Christian Endeavor organization, I have come to know very intimately the ministers of the American Christian Convention, and to honor them as a noble band of devout, earnest, sweet-spirited Christians, ably leading a host of the same beautiful character as themselves. In honoring today our oldest religious newspaper, we do honor also to the ministers and churches that have supported it all through this century, and are putting into it today their ever-new enthusiasm for what is highest and best.

I trust you will pardon these personal words.

I am to speak to you for a few minutes on "Religious Journal-

[1] Delivered on Wednesday morning, September 16th, in the M.E. church. Mr. Wells represented *The Christian Endeavor World,* Boston, Mass.

ism for the Young." We are here today to express our regard for what is old—one hundred years old. And yet it is eminently appropriate that we should devote some time to thinking of our young people. It is the spirit of eternal youth which we honor in the *Herald of Gospel Liberty*. It is more sprightly now, more wide-awake, more virile, than ever before in all its hundred years of useful life. If it were not so, we should have little heart in this centennial. The birthdays of decrepit old age are melancholy. The birthdays of children and youth are full of inspiration and cheer.

But the *Herald of Gospel Liberty* is renewing its youth in large part because the young are now trained, as never before, to value the church and all its institutions, including its printed journals. A church of the mature or the aged lacks everything but experience. It is the church into which the young pour their ever-fresh reinforcements of courage and hope and enthusiasm that reaches its centennial anniversaries with vigor and renown.

I am no pessimist. The churches are doing far more than ever before toward the training of their youth, in whom lies their hope for the winning of the world to Christ. With every glad year of this Twentieth Century the churches will. I am sure, do more for the religious education of the young. I could not remain in the Christian Endeavor work and not be an optimist in this regard.

But, nevertheless, I want to raise here the question whether the churches have yet even begun to realize the value of religious periodicals for the young, still less have begun to utilize those periodicals as they should.

I think that, on consideration, that question must be answered in the negative.

So far as the reading of our young people goes, the secularites have their way in most households. Almost without exception, the distinctive young people's periodicals, those of widest circulation, largest means, and greatest influence, are not religious periodicals. Of course, they are not irreligious. Many of them are edited by religious men. They are all pure and moral in their tone, if we except the detective story papers and their like. These are sold by the million copies every week and their influence is distinctly Satanic; but Christian parents are on the watch against them, and I am talking about the periodicals for which Christian parents subscribe. Those periodicals are moral, but not religious.

That is, while they paint pictures of national heroes and try to develop patriotism, they do not point to the God of nations, or show how in the teachings of Christ lies the hope of national welfare. They may have articles on Tennyson, but not on Paul; on Shakespeare, but not on the Bible. They discuss the latest discoveries of science, but not in such a way as to exalt the God of nature. They teach industry, but not prayerfulness. They inculcate honesty, but not repentance of sin. The goal they hold up before the young man is getting on in the world, and not getting on toward heaven. The heroes they picture are Washington, and Lincoln, and Cromwell, and Gladstone, but they leave out the greatest hero of all, our Lord Jesus Christ. In short, these periodicals give our young folks the case, and face, and hands, and cogs of conduct, but entirely omit the mainspring.

Now the periodical read by a boy or girl has a vast influence upon his or her destiny. I well remember how my entire boyhood and young manhood were directed by *Our Young Folks,* and *The Little Corporal,* and *The Schoolday Magazine,* and *St. Nicholas.* Noble and inspiring magazines, every one of them, and I owe them a great debt of gratitude; but I grew up wholly ignorant of the claims of Christ upon my heart and life, wholly ignorant of the triumphs of the church on the mission field and its tremendous work in the modern world. My introduction to all that came through my joining the Christian Endeavor society and reading its paper, then *The Golden Rule.* If it had not been for that influence, my life would have been secularized instead of spiritualized.

The century covered by the *Herald of Gospel Liberty* has seen vast progress in reading matter for the young. *The Youth's Companion,* established in 1826 by Nathaniel Willis, was a pioneer in this great field, and worthily holds the ground today with undiminished energy and Influence. But the chief growth has come within the last twenty-five years. I have been looking over some files of the Sunday-school papers that I received in my boyhood days, and I am amazed to note the cheap paper on which they are printed, the worn-out woodcuts made to do second service therein, and the uninteresting and mechanical character of the contents. I well remember the advent of a better type of Sunday-school paper, instinct with life, the stories dealing in a natural way with natural boys and girls, and the pages filled with bright accounts of real men and events and things. Those papers Were eagerly read in my school, absentees were careful to call for the numbers they had missed, and a genuine influence over lives began to be exerted.

From that day to the present, the Sunday-school papers for children have experienced an evolution that is both delightful and remarkable. The best writers obtainable now contribute to their pages. Admirable artists draw their pictures. Good paper and good printing make them a joy to the eye and the hand. The editors are among our country's most cultured and wide-awake men and women. The Sunday-school library has undergone a metamorphosis even more surprising, but that is outside the theme of this address. To say that a book or paper is "Sunday-schooly" is no longer a term of just reproach.

While this advance has taken place, the departments of our religious papers for adults that had been set apart for the children have suffered a decline; or, at the best, they have stood still. In some of our leading religious papers, such as *The Outlook* and *The Independent,* they have been abandoned altogether. Those that retain these departments place them in the back of the paper next to the advertisements, and make them up largely with a pair of shears and a mucilage bottle. You could name on the fingers of one hand the religious papers that put any amount of original skill and thoughtful planning into the editing of their departments for children.

I am inclined to think that this is wise and inevitable. It is simply a recognition of the fact that the elders do not want their papers taken up with juvenile matter, and of the further fact that the children are coming to be well supplied with separate periodicals of their own. It is merely one more indication of the specializing tendency of the age.

But while the Sunday-school has been improving the character of its periodicals, other religious organizations have not been idle. The temperance societies now issue admirable papers, calculated to interest young folks in that great movement. Societies for the prevention of cruelty to animals, rightly seeing the need of instructing boys and girls, if they would make any progress in their reform, are sending forth brightly written and excellently published periodicals. Many of the missionary boards now appeal to the young folks with very attractive monthlies, well calculated to win their hearts for the greatest work of the church. Above all, as is proper, the young people's religious societies, both the interdenominational Christian Endeavor Society and the various denominational societies like the Epworth League, the Baptist Young People's Union, and the Luther League, not to forget the King's Daughters and the Young Men's Christian Association and the Boys' Brigade, are issuing weeklies and monthlies for young folks that are rapidly approaching, if they do not already equal, the best that the religious press can furnish for their elders. These are bewildering in their number and variety. There are, for example, about two dozen Christian Endeavor papers published in the United States alone. Surely, so far as quantity is concerned, the amount of capital invested and the number of bright brains at work, the young people of this generation need not complain of their religious periodicals.

But has the ideal yet been reached? No, indeed! Neither, for that matter, has it been reached by the editors and publishers of religious periodicals for adults. Perhaps the one set of papers is as near the ideal, on the whole, as the other. Let me take a few minutes to set forth what that ideal is, as it lies in my own mind.

In the first place, negatively, the ideal religious periodical for young people must be absolutely pure. Its stories must be free from suggestion of any evil, its editorials must be sound in theology and crystal-clear in morals, its writers must be men and women of high character, its language must be chaste and refined, in every way it must be without reproach. The paper is to become a very real and intimate friend of every young reader. It must be a friend that never betrays into iniquity or even a fault.

This negative virtue is as far as many go in estimating a religious periodical for the youth. "Is it good?" they ask, forgetting to inquire whether, being good, it is also good for anything. It is possible for a paper to be as pure as snow, and at the same time it may be as cold as snow. It is not the ideal, by any means, until the editor has poured into it the warm, red blood of abounding life.

And so, I must go on to speak in a positive and not merely a negative way of what the ideal religious periodical for young people should contain. I can put it in a single word: Christ! If the periodical shows its readers Christ, the living Christ, now at work in and for the world, and if it shows Him in His fullness, I shall be satisfied with it That is my own aim as editor of such a periodical. It is the aim of every editor of a religious paper worthy of his exalted trust.

But what do I mean by an exhibition of the living Christ in His fullness? Very much such an exhibition as Paul meant when he said that it was his purpose to be all things to all men. It is required of these periodicals of which 1 am speaking that they be all things —all Christian things— to all young people.

For one thing, they must show Christ in nature. We are living in an age when Christ in nature, the Creator Christ, is coming to be understood as never before. He is disclosing some of His most marvelous secrets, and young people are quick to respond to the marvel of them when they are presented. The ideal religious periodical for the young of today will have much to say of the telephone and the telegraph and their wonderful development; of electric cars, and electric lights and electric heaters; of the phonograph, and the telephotograph and the microscope; of the telescope and the spectroscope; of wireless telegraphy, and automobiles and flying machines; of chemistry, and surgery, and biology and astronomy. Every word in that list is eloquent of Christ and His infinitely wise plans for His creatures. To relate the wonders of science, as the secular periodicals do, and leave Christ out of them, is to tell our children about the locomotive, but remain silent concerning the steam. Thus, also they are taught in most of their schools, and there is the greatest need that they should have one periodical that, while picturing these disclosures in all their amazing strangeness, should clearly point the reader to their loving and majestic Source. This is no slight service that the young people's religious periodical will perform if it is true to its high calling in Christ Jesus.

And then, besides showing Christ in nature, the ideal religious periodical for young folks will show Christ in history, in the history of the past, but more especially in the events of the present world. Very early, nowadays, the young people are initiated into newspaper-reading. The Sunday newspaper, with its vicious comic supplement especially for children, is taken in millions of homes, and many of them are the homes of church-members. What a picture of the world is presented by the average newspaper! It is a world of flaunting vice and sneering selfishness. Politics is represented as a game of grab. Society is painted as a reeking sore. Sport is a vast gamble. The sun rises upon murders and thefts and sets upon scandal and shame. It is a world of sordidness and vulgarity and abominable sin, the world of the average newspaper.

But the boy and girl are rightly curious about this great, fresh world around them. Their public school makes them intensely awake to what is going on in the world. Their teachers send them to the newspapers for illustrations of their geography and history. They are bound to get an initiation into life, and as soon as possible; if not the right kind of life, then the wrong kind. Is it not plain that one of the outstanding needs of childhood and youth is for a religious newspaper, a paper that will present current events in a Christian manner and from the Christian view-point?

Therefore, the ideal religious paper for the young must be a newspaper. It must have a wide view of the world. It must be able to get the just proportion of events. Every week, amid all the crimes and sensational disasters and pitiless gossip that crowd our dailies, something happens, usually many things happen, that are genuine mileposts in the progress of mankind. These events, often unnoticed by the secular newspaper, are the real news of the day. They are full of thrilling interest, to one that is actually awake to the things of time and eternity. It is the duty and the joy of the religious editor to set them forth before the bright eyes of his young readers in their true colors and their inspiring possibilities.

Foremost among these events, of course, are the triumphs of the cross upon mission fields, at home and abroad. Missionaries and pastors are hardly mentioned in the newspapers, unless one of them goes wrong in some sensational way or makes some sensational reference to politics. The religious editor sees in them, and in the philanthropists and charitable workers of the day, the real heroes and heroines of current history, and in their accomplishments the chief history of the times. Every young people's periodical must be a missionary paper, if it is to approach the ideal.

It goes without saying that if the periodical for youth is to exhibit Christ in history, it will have much to say about our nation. It will be intensely patriotic, but not in the narrow and contemptible sense that consists chiefly in brag, that exalts our own land at the expense of all other countries. Pride is not patriotism. Indeed, when our country is wrong, shame is the only possible patriotism. Patriotism is the home sense, and it is never possible to have a home sense till one has wisely traveled abroad. Just as the family is happiest that loves other families the most and does its best to help them in their sorrows and share in their joys, so that nation is happiest whose citizens admire other countries also, and are eager to help them in their trials and take part in their rejoicings. In this spirit, then, the young people's paper will study its own land. make its readers familiar with her leaders and their aims, and the methods of government and conduct of business. While the words of the average newspaper tend to manufacture partisans and fanatics and Jingoes, the religious newspaper for the young should aim to produce among its readers, nay, in every reader, that rare and splendid individual, a cosmopolitan patriot.

And in the third place, while showing Christ in nature and in history, the ideal religious paper for the young will show Christ in the work of the world. Its editor must not for a moment forget that he is addressing ambitious and rightly ambitious readers. We cannot be sure that they are interested in the way of salvation, but we may be certain that they are eager to know the way to get on in the world. There is a widely-read paper for youth that rejoices in the attractive name, *"Success"* Every religious paper for the young might well adopt the same name as a sub-head. Every religious newspaper must deal largely, if it is to meet the needs of its readers, with the proper ambitions of the young, their desire to impress themselves upon the world and get from the world what they want to get.

But this is already done for the young in many periodicals, an increasing number, done with great skill and practical wisdom. Yes; but the religious periodical must do it differently! It must show Christ and not Mammon as the guiding spirit in all work that is worth while. It *must* make it perfectly clear that, while wealth is a *good thing,* it is not by any manner of means the best thing. While it points out the way to wealth, it must show that there are ways to wealth that are at the same time the ways to misery and perdition. It must so work upon its readers that rather than take a million dollars in certain ways they would cut off their hands. It must exhibit certain failures, as the world regards them, in such an aspect that they will be seen to be the most radiant successes; and certain successes, as the world regards them, in such a light that they will be recognized as the most deplorable failures. The ideal young people's religious paper will be as practical as any trade paper. It will talk about definite businesses, and will give first-hand and businesslike information regarding them. It will inspire young people to succeed in them. It will show them how to make money, how to save it, and how to invest it. But it will not allow them, while they are making money, to unmake manhood, or, while they are saving it, to forget to spend it wisely and generously for the needs of others and in the love of Christ.

Without Christ in our work that work soon loses all just proportion in our thoughts; it becomes a work for time and not for eternity; for ourselves and not for the world; for loss and not for real prosperity. Most influences, in secular schools, in secular periodicals, and in the well-nigh overpowering spirit of the age, utterly omit Christ from the work of the world, and from the training of the young for that work. Is it not plain that the religious periodical for young people has here a rich field of service, and a field that greatly needs enthusiastic cultivation?

Further, the religious periodical for young folks must put Christ into their play as well as their work. It must show them how to play in wise ways. More persons know how to work than how to play. With all the miles of columns about sport published daily in our newspapers there are very few inches that really help the world toward genuine recreation. Now the need of recreation runs parallel to the need of work, and if young people are to be taught one, they should be taught the other. It is my belief that considerable space in the ideal religious periodical for the young should be occupied with descriptions of sensible amusements—what they are, how to play them, and when to stop playing them. Many of these should be amusements for large parties, and not the somewhat selfish games for two or four, or those foolish games that are enjoyed by proxy, as when ten thousand persons sit on benches to watch twenty-two persons play.

I believe the religious paper should have large space for fun, for those comical sayings and happenings that expel miasmas with a laugh, and drive away the devil with chuckles. I believe, too, that much attention should be given to the social aspect of life, and especially to that matter of paramount importance to the young, love-making and marriage. Bodily purity and all that that implies should be a part of this constant propaganda. One widely circulated paper for young folks used to rule out all stories of religion and of love; I think it does still. To my mind, wise stories of religion and of love, the two combined, are ideally appropriate for the. young peoples' periodical.

Well, there is much more that I should like to say on this outreaching theme, and certainly I do not want it understood * that my omission of any point implies that I do not consider it important; but the time is short. Perhaps I can put the most of what I want to say in a single additional statement, that the ideal religious periodical for youth will aim to put Christ in their hearts. Christ in nature and in history, Christ in work and in play, but most of all Christ in the heart. Personal love for Christ, personal consecration to Christ, personal service of Christ, —to bring this about must be the editor's crowning aim. He must think of this as he plans every number. He must think of this as he selects his writers and passes upon their manuscripts. He must think of this as he writes his editorials. He must place this first as he daily brings his paper and his readers before the throne of God in prayer. He must send forth every number as a printed John the Baptist, to prepare the way of the Lord. He must consider the paper as his pulpit and himself as a minister of the gospel. And as he does this, and every other man engaged in the same blessed work does this, his living enthusiasm will be caught up by the eager and receptive souls of the young; they will come to see Christ as the One Desire of all nations; they will begin to pour into His royal service the full tide of their splendid energy and devotion, and before long Christ's kingdom will come upon earth. For whatever touches and molds youth decides the eternal destiny of mankind.

THE MORAL INFLUENCE OF RELIGIOUS JOURNALISM

BY REV. A.C. YOUMANS[1]

There is a great temptation to enter into the making of definitions, to state what we mean by morals and religion. There are so many different conceptions of both, and so many theories as to the source and development thereof, that it might not be altogether a waste of time to state what we mean by the terms of our subject.

Many may be found that make morals the custodian of religion, who hold that morals as a phenomenon of life appeared before the religious sense.

Often, we see them treated as distinct and separate things; but we feel that as a man is a unit in his soul life, and that we may not take any one power thereof and hold it as apart from the other; so, man in his religious and moral life must be looked at as a unit, the same source for the ethical as for the religious phenomena and impulses.

Some will not admit of any *a priori* arguments: they have no place for the proposition that there is a God who reigneth; and they look upon religion as a fetish. Not God, but a "fortuitous concourse of atoms" has been the source of this development which we have seen as recorded in the history of civilization.

Have we not looked on both sides of the question and by the processes of philosophy, and through our experiences arrived at the same conclusions as Descartes, who found that next to the most obvious thing in the universe— "I think, therefore I am." is that "there is a God who is the secret of my ability to think."

We feel that we may not divorce morals from religion. Said Wash-

---

[1] Delivered on Wednesday morning. Sept ember 16th. in the M.E. church. Mr. Youmans is pastor of the First Christian church, Albany, N.Y.

ington.

> Let us with caution indulge the supposition that morality can be maintained without religion. Reason and experience both forbid us to expect that natural morality can prevail in exclusion of religious principles.

The same eternal cause, God, is producing them both, and we may not have a pure religious state without a right system of morals, and vice versa.

To us who believe in God and the eternal value of religion, our subject is simple enough. In the form of a question it means, — "What influence has religious journalism on the conduct of man?"

Nothing more decidedly emphasized the moral value of religious journalism than does the MOTIVE under which it is carried on. The secular press appears to be run upon an egoistic basis. One question is asked, "Will it pay?" By pay is meant, will it prosper financially, and pay large dividends to the entrepreneurs? Or may be, "will it serve the end of a party or class?" Commercialism, class and individual interests seem to be the motives under the secular press today.

On the other hand, the religious press is a philanthropic enterprise. The motive is altruistic. Seldom does it meet with financial success. If I am rightly informed the larger numbers of religious periodicals have to be subsidized. The question is not what can be gotten out of it, but what can be done by putting into it.

As motive is seen to be the basic element in morals, we see that the religious press stands before the world in a white light, and is armed with the invincibleness of sincerity and simplicity and charged with the power of the spirit of benevolence.

Next to the motive we might examine the PURPOSE. What is its aim? The aim is the reclamation, the salvation, the edification of man.

It does not seek to simply please, to amuse and be sold; but it goes to man as Old Nathan the prophet did to David to tell him of his sin and to point the finger of conviction at him while he declared "thou art the man." It is aimed at the conscience of man seeking to make it alive and free and regnant.

In the business world man is surrounded with so many things which smother the conscience; in the political arena so many things that lead him into the attitude of a casuist; in the social realm so much to make him turn from inner promptings, which tend to put in abeyance the voice of the divine in his soul, that there needs to be something to make a special appeal to him from time to *time. This is* what the truly religious journal does.

The religious press seeks the heart of man. It strives to stir the emotions; not as the play on the stage, or the novel in the hand, which are for the passing moment's effect only, and to be lost in the next picture of life that is seen, thus leaving the heart less impressionable. The religious writer has not as the end in view the emotion, the tear; but seeks out of these to get conviction and a decision, with resolutions which shall change the life. He writes not as an entertainer so much as a reformer and inspirer of man.

Another characteristic of religious journalism is its spirit of truth. It seeks to set forth the *truth.* We do not mean by this that it always contains truth in the absolute, in the last analysis; but the writing has been done in simplicity and sincerity.

The creed of one paper may not be that of another, the writings of one may differ in opinions from those of another on the opposite page. Yet we feel that each out of the earnest of his spirit has set forth that which appeared as eternal truth to him. There is an absence of the politic, the subterfuge, the diplomacy, the legerdemain that so disgusts us in the secular press.

We are convinced that the writers are men with the interest of humanity at heart, and they are not writing their articles because it pays in dollars, but because of the spirit of eureka within them, and because they feel woe is me if I declare not the truth.

The spirit which is thus revealed by such, calls men to sincerity, away from the temptation to put things in an illusory light.

The religious press holds up the better side of life. The dailies ransack the whole earth to find all the rapine, murder, theft and crime, taking the whisperings of every scandal monger and with the imagination of a Jules Verne or a Rider Haggard paint them in a fairy tale of fiction giving it to the public as fact.

If two derelicts of humanity fight on the street, there will be a two-column article. All the prize fights and dog fights are the things which they seek after the most, and serve up with the greatest satisfaction.

When did you see them publish anything when a Nathaniel under the fig tree, or a Jacob at Penuel, or any man fought and conquered the demons of his soul? Such news is spurned by them.

The religious press comes in here to tell of the soul's conquests, to give us the view of life from some spiritual height obtained. To reveal to man a way out of his discouragement, his weakness, his sin.

In the secular press we have the lower side of life spread before us each day. To read this alone would make man a pessimist as touching humanity, and complacent with himself, for "surely he is better than these."

In the religious press we see the other side; we get a fairer view of man, which makes us optimistic as touching the outcome of the race, and makes us dissatisfied with our own poor attainment in things spiritual, when we see the souls of great men shining out through their writings and works. The highest ideals are held up before man with encouragement for him to strive after them, while evidences that men have attained are placed before him in abundance.

How different the ideas of success as held out by the two classes of journalism. Croesus and Napoleon are the patron saints of the many who write for man in the popular periodicals. "Get up and on" is their slogan, while materialistic means and ends are as far as they see to go.

Here the religious periodical comes to our homes and assures us that it is not success to walk over the prostrated bodies of our compatriots and fellowmen to reach our desired ends; that when we must build up our homes and fortunes at the expense of the homes and fortunes of others ; when our achievements are bathed with the *blood of* victims, instead of being baptized with honest *perspiration* from our own brows; be it that in gold we represent a Croesus, or in power a Caesar, we have failed; and though in the house of Dagon we may have mounted to great heights among the world gods, we shall surely be thrown down before the presence of

Him who requires that we "do justly, love mercy and walk humbly before him."

The Man of Galilee came to the people of Palestine in His day teaching that the meek shall inherit the earth, that a man's life consisteth not in the material things which he possesses, that one should not live by bread alone, that faith hope and love are the only things abiding; so, the religious press born of His spirit declares the same principles.

The world has that which they call faith or confidence, but the religious press lifts faith into the realm of the spirit, it takes hope through the vistas of the eternal morn. It elevates love from the realm of selfishness and sex into the impersonal, unifying, glorifying realm of Love Divine.

What a unifying power is the religious press? It points all men to one center, —God the beginning, the end, the all. With God as the core of a moral system there will be advancement in things ethical. With God left out there will be false and arbitrary centers which work apart and can lead only to deterioration and depravity. Religion is not a handmaiden of a materialistic system of ethics. Religion is paternal and declares to all men and systems the God that has been experienced. A father has been comprehended and as his children have found true life lies along his ways, they will seek the counsels of his spirit, even more than the rules of any ethical system. Religious experience will make and remake these systems, even as it makes and remakes theology.

There is much complaint that there is not so much Bible study as in the past, that there is not so much reading of the text itself, by Christians. I suspect that the religious press is partly responsible for the fact that there is not so much reading of the book itself. When a person reads from one to five religious periodicals a week, he has read a great deal of Bible in a very good way. The periodicals are saturated with the Bible texts, and some of the most excellent expositions of texts and paragraphs are given by men of rich experience and deep religious insight. In this way the average man gets a better understanding of the Bible than he would by simply reading it himself. He is studying the Bible in detail.

The Influence of religious journalism? It is beneficent, stimulating, redeeming. When a periodical is sent forth without any self-interest back of it, but sprung from divine love in the human heart; when it bears a message of faith service, sacrifice and immortality; when it ever holds on high the crucified, the beatified Christ, it is a light shining in the darkness, a force countering the gross and material, it is leaven in the loaf of life, which tends to permeate the heart of the individual, the home, the community, the world. It is "the voice of one crying in the wilderness, prepare ye the way of the Lord, make his paths straight."

It is no small honor to the Christians that they were the first to see the great need and set about supplying it, as they did by initiating the new form of journalism which has grown to such wonderful proportions.

A hundred years of service to man through the means of the printed page! When we agree with one who said: "The pen is mightier than the sword," are we not amazed at the influence that has been exerted through the century? If we could see the mighty host that our own paper has helped, the ones who have been led to the light of a new day, the ones encouraged in their darker moments, those who by the reading of the timely paragraph have been stayed from the great transgression; if we could estimate the amount of edification, character building that has been the result of the influence of the *Herald of Gospel Liberty*, we should take up the cause of the paper with a thousand-fold increase in zeal.

I would pay my own respects to the *Herald*. It was the first paper I remember seeing in our home. Never during all the years that I remained under *the parental* roof did it miss its weekly visit. Ours was *not a wealthy* home, and at times the *Herald* was the only paper coming therein. The library was small, the books were Biblical and theological with the exception of a few histories and one novel, "Thaddeus of Warsaw." By force I read the books and the one periodical, the *Herald*. It was in the days when Doctor Watson was editor that I began to read it. What sweet breaths of the Spirit he blew into the paper. I can now feel the impressions that they made upon my boyish heart. I have often thanked God that it was as it was, and that I did not read the mass and the mess that is obtainable today. With the *Herald. Geikie's Life of Christ and Kinkade's Bible Doctrine* I spent many an hour in my boyhood, and to this I, in a large measure, attribute the bent of my life.

Today there are probably twenty-five periodicals coming into our home. The first read is the *Herald*. It has not diminished in its power, its influence, its potency for righteousness, but rather increased.

Religious journalism was born of necessity, it has enlarged the pulpit thousand-fold, it has made the home more the house of the Lord, and its mission will not have been accomplished until that time shall be which the seer of the apocalypse declared, when no temple shall be needed, neither shall the preacher exhort, for all shall know the Lord from the least unto the greatest.

UNITARIAN CHURCH
Where Wednesday Afternoon Session was held.

A HISTORICAL SKETCH OF THE MORNING STAR
COMPILED AND READ BY
REV. G.C. WATERMAN[1]

On the 30th of June, 1780, the Rev. Benjamin Randall, a "free salvation" Baptist preacher, organized in the town of New Durham, N.H., an independent Baptist church, called the "Church of Christ," and that church constituted "the germ" of what is now known as the "Free Baptist" denomination. Randall did not accept the extreme Calvinistic doctrines commonly held and preached in

the Baptist denomination at that time; he believed and boldly preached the freedom* of the human will, a general atonement, and man's responsibility for his relation to his Creator, and also in the right of all true disciples to the privileges of the Lord's Table. Other preachers agreed with him in these views, and gradually they gathered churches in different places, which, as might be expected, accepted the same doctrines. For more than twenty years they called themselves simply "Baptist" churches, but were not looked upon favorably in the denomination, and were spoken of as "New Lights," and sometimes as "Free Willers;" and other discourteous names were applied to them. Naturally they associated with one another, and soon began to form alliances, or associations, and in 1804 were recognized in law, *by* action of the New Hampshire legislature, as the "Freewill Antipedo Baptist Church and Society." At that time, so far as is known, no religious newspaper had been published on either side of the Atlantic. The earliest publication of this kind was the *Herald of Gospel Liberty*, published at Portsmouth,

---

[1] Delivered on Wednesday afternoon, September 16th, in the Unitarian church. Mr. Waterman represented the *Morning Star,* organ of the Free Baptists, of Boston, Mass.

N.H., the first number appearing September 8, 1808. In it the editor remarks:

> "A religious newspaper is almost a new thing under the sun. I know not but this is the first ever published to the world."

Freewill Baptists were, to some extent, interested in this earliest religious newspaper. Its founder and first editor, the Rev. Elias Smith, sought admission, in 1805, into the Freewill Baptist denomination, but finding himself not fully in accord with their doctrines, he withdrew his request, but continued to associate with them in the most unrestrained manner. The sympathy of Freewill Baptists was with this paper in its leading designs, and it had quite an extensive circulation among them.

In 1811, the Rev. John Buzzell, of North Parsonsfield, Me., began to publish a quarterly periodical called *The Religious Magazine,* which appeared in 1811-12, and then disappeared until 1820, when it re-appeared and was continued for three years. It was filled with historical, biographical and denominational intelligence, and may, in some sense, be regarded as the forerunner of the *Morning Star,* as its founder and editor were one of the founders and the first editor of the *Star.*

The history of the *Morning Star* may not improperly be regarded as beginning with the appearance of *The Religious Magazine* in 1811; for that was the earlier expression of a purpose that afterwards was permanently realized in the appearance of *The Morning Star.* The naan who originated and conducted the first was one of the founders of the second. Elder John Buzzell was one of the three men who, in 1825, first consulted the Parsonsfield Quarterly Meeting on the subject of a weekly paper. Buzzell was also one of the original stockholders *and the first* editor-in-chief of the *Star.*

In 1826 the Freewill Baptists numbered nearly four hundred churches, over three hundred ministers, and about sixteen thousand communicants. These were scattered throughout New England (Connecticut excepted), New York, Pennsylvania, Ohio, Indiana, and Canada. The need of a weekly paper had come to be deeply felt. What was really needed by a body that had quadrupled its membership in two decades could not be long delayed. In 1825 Samuel Burbank and Elias Libby agreed to consult the Parsonfield Quarterly Meeting at its next session as to the expediency of publishing a paper. They did so (Elder John Buzzell being associated with them), and the Quarterly Meeting doubted its success, but agreed to patronize it if commenced. Nine men were found ready to assume the publication of a paper. They commenced with a capital of $800 and issued their prospectus Jan. 2, 1826. The company was not legally organized till Feb. 4, when the articles of co-partnership (under the name of Hobbs, Woodman & Co.) were signed. Hobbs was chosen chairman, and Burbank clerk. Arrangements were then made for procuring a press, type, paper, etc., and, at a subsequent meeting John Buzzell was chosen senior editor, and Samuel Burbank resident editor and agent; William Burr, a young man about twenty years of age, then in the *Traveller* office at Boston, was engaged as printer. The type for the first paper was mostly set with his own hand, and *May 11, 1826,* was issued the first number of *The Morning Star.* It was published at Limerick, Me., a small village thirty miles from Portland, and about the same distance from Dover, N.H., to which place it was removed seven years later.

The *Star* was actually opposed by some on the ground that it would foster pride, stimulate a false ambition, or be a money-making speculation. The second number contains a dialogue, substantially representing conversations between the editor and those who doubted the propriety of establishing a weekly paper, in which the wisdom of the movement is fully vindicated. To satisfy objectors, at the end of the first six months, it was editorially announced that the proprietors were ready to transfer the *Star* to the denomination whenever it would take the paper and pay the bills. Any Quarterly Meeting dissatisfied with the financial management was asked to send a committee of investigation, and the agent would submit all of his books and accounts for examination. These offers seemed to have silenced the grumblers.

At the commencement of the second volume only six subscribers had discontinued the paper. At the first General Conference of the denomination, held at Tunbridge, Vt, in 1827, the object of the proprietors in establishing *The Morning Star* was fully explained and the paper with all the office appliances, was offered to the denomination at cost. The offer was declined, but the *Star* was commended to the patronage of the denomination. In the middle of the third volume, with a subscription list of 1250, the Star was enlarged, and in 1830 William Burr was appointed financial agent and held that office till his death, nearly thirty-seven years afterwards.

At the General Conference in 1832 the proprietors of the *Star* again offered it for sale, and the Conference agreed to pay $3,700 for all the property. The publishing committee consisted of six men, with David Marks as publishing agent, William Burr still retaining the office management. A new interest was awakened, and the subscription list of 1,600 increased the next year to 2,700. No change was made in the editorial management.

Two important changes occurred in 1833. After seven years of faithful service in the editorial chair, Rev. Samuel Burbank vacated it, carrying with him the best wishes of the thousands who had read the paper. Samuel Beede, of Sandwich, N.H., a very pious and scholarly young man, who had been in the employ of the Book Concern for a year or more, was his successor, and he soon showed himself equal to the task. Beede and Burr were kindred spirits, and worked harmoniously together.

The inconveniences of publishing the *Star* and books in a retired place like Limerick became more and more apparent as the business increased, and so the publishing Committee proposed to the General Conference, in 1833. that the publication office be removed to a more eligible location; and the Conference recommended its removal to Dover, N.H., which was affected a few weeks after. But Beede's service was brief. His real worth was beginning to be appreciated when he was called to a higher service, and died March 28, 1834, after a short illness, and the *Star* was dressed in mourning for the first time. In May Mr. Burr was chosen office editor, with the understanding that he would use at his discretion the editorials furnished by others, and Arthur Caverno, David Marks, Porter S. Burbank, John J. Butler and Enock Mack were appointed assistant editors.

The bold and uncompromising position of the *Star* against slavery disaffected many subscribers, and the orders for its discontinuance came every day. Brethren said that the managers were acting a suicidal part, and ought to keep silence on that exciting question, and politicians and the press generally denounced the anti-slavery policy of the *Star*. The New Hampshire legislature refused to give the trustees an act of incorporation, and they were pressed on every side, but not discouraged. Those were the dark days of the Book Concern. Men of less heroic principle would have quailed before the storm; but the *Star* shone with a steady light for free speech and free men through all of those terrible years. The Lord was pleased with the service, and crowned it with success. The General Conference stood by the *Star,* giving it hearty sympathy and words of cheer, and the ministry, with few exceptions, worked for it with a hearty good-will.

In 1844 the Concern was enabled to report itself as having an office of its own, with greatly increased facilities for carrying on the work, and, best of all, it was free from debt. Then commenced large appropriations of $1,500 annually to benevolent purposes, in addition to some larger and all the minor donations.

In 1846 a political revolution was affected in New Hampshire, and an act of incorporation obtained. The board of corporators, thirteen in number, organized Sept. 30 under the legal title of "The Freewill Baptist Printing Establishment," and all the property held by the trustees was duly transferred.

The next twenty years (1846-1866) were years of prosperity and progress. The entire denomination was then united in support of the *Star;* the subscription list ran up to more than 12,000, and the profits enabled the Board, under the direction of Conference, to make large and repeated donations to worthy objects.

The *Star* was again enlarged in 1851. In 1864 the Rev. J.M. Brewster entered the office as assistant in the editorial department, and in 1866 Mr. Burr was suddenly called away by death. Then was there great sorrow throughout the denomination, for one of the best men and most useful servants it has ever produced had "entered into rest"

The Rev. George T. Day was elected editor to succeed Mr. Burr, and the Rev. Silas Curtis was made temporary agent. He was relieved in the next year by Mr. L.R. Burlingame.

In 1867 it was decided to enlarge the *Star* again, and to publish it in quarto form. This made necessary the purchase of a new press and folder, additional appliances, and the other half of the building in which it was published, one-half of which it had owned for several years.

At the Buffalo session of the General Conference, in 1868, a somewhat radical change in the affairs of the Printing Establishment was affected. The corporators were directed "to obtain such an alteration in their act of incorporation, and make such changes in their by-laws, as will remove the said Printing Establishment from the control of the General Conference." The object of this measure was in various ways to conserve the interests of the Establishment and secure its greater efficiency. The capital of the Establishment was to be "placed absolutely under the control of the corporators . . . not to be subject to the interference of General Conference, to be used for the publication of such books and periodicals as said corporators may deem advisable, and that all profits arising- from the business shall be appropriated to benevolent purposes connected with the denomination, except when such profits may *be* required as capital for the publication of books."

The question of moving the publishing office to Boston had been discussed for some time, and in 1874 it was voted to do so. But removal was not yet to occur. Dr. Day was taken sick and soon passed away. His death and other circumstances prevented carrying into effect the vote to remove. All steps in that direction were retraced except rescinding the vote to move, and the *Star* remained in its old home. Mr. Geo. F. Mosher, who had been in the office several years as Mr. Day's assistant, succeeded him as editor. In 1881, Mr. Mosher resigned and went abroad as United States Consul to Nice, to which position he had been appointed by President Garfield. The Rev. Clarence A. Bickford was then chosen editor, and in a letter to the Board of Corporators, re-opened the question of removal. At the meeting of the Corporators, in Sept., 1883, it was voted to proceed with the proposed removal, and that was accomplished in 1885.

With the removal of the Establishment to Boston there occurred, through the resignation of Rev. I.D. Stewart, a complete change in the business management. He was succeeded by Rev. E.N. Fernald, to whose care, as chairman of the executive committee of the Board, the work of building in Boston was largely entrusted. No change occurred in the editorial management, save the retirement of Rev. G.C. Waterman, who for some years had conducted the *Star Quarterlies* and the Sunday-school papers. The necessity of retrenchment, owing to increased expenses in Boston, called for a reduction in the working force. All the publications were now placed in the hands of the Rev. C.A. Bickford, as editor-in-chief, assisted by Prof. Cyrus Jordan and Miss Sarah A. Perkins. Dr. Bickford served as editor till Nov. 1, 1901, when he was succeeded by the Hon. George F. Mosher, who is the present editor and publisher.

Previous to its removal to Boston, the Publishing House was a source of large pecuniary profit to the denomination. More than $80,000 in money, or its equivalent, has been received from the House, in addition to all the stimulating social, moral and religious influence it has exerted, without giving to it a single donation. No Institution has done more for Free Baptists or has a greater claim upon their patronage.

The position of the *Star* in relation to slavery has been noticed. It was from the beginning a firm and zealous advocate of the temperance reform, and is today an uncompromising defender of Prohibition. When the denomination began to be definitely interested in Foreign Missions, the *Star* gave efficient help to, and direction in, the work. It has assisted greatly in awakening and maintaining an intelligent interest in educational matters, in Sunday- schools, and in the Young People's Societies. It maintains a reasonably conservative attitude towards the modern developments in respect to biblical and theological questions and is a progressive leader in all evangelistic movements, both within the denomination and the general Christian community.

THE DEVELOPMENT OF BAPTIST JOURNALISM
BY REV. JOSEPH S. SWAIM[1]

Baptist Journalism may be traced to 1790 when the *Baptist Annual Register* was established in England by Dr. John Ripon, successor to Doctor Gill in the church in Southwark, London. This publication included communications from Americans also and was a means of communication sufficient for their simple purposes at that early stage of the American churches.

In 1803 the *Massachusetts Baptist Missionary Magazine* appeared as the organ of foreign missionary intelligence. The missionary enterprise knit the Baptists together and developed a desire for communication of knowledge of all their interests. It might be expected that Baptists would take an early interest in journalism, as they were active in propagating their faith by preaching and the publication of pamphlets, and found also the need of educational institutions to prepare ministers. They became a thoughtful people, and as such, needed journals of information and expression.

Pamphlets and periodicals on doctrinal and denominational subjects were first issued. But as their numbers and activities increased and as they came to the period of self-consciousness as a growing denomination of Christians, they felt the necessity of a religious journal which would serve their common interests.

Our topic calls for "Journalism" and we must confine our story to weekly religious publications, leaving out doctrinal and denominational pamphlets and books, as well as missionary magazines, and condensing history and outstanding facts.

[1] Delivered on Wednesday afternoon, September 16th, in the Unitarian church. Mr. Swaim represented *The Watchman,* of Boston, Mass.

Taking up the thread at actual and bonafide weekly publications of newspapers, we find that the *Watchman* first appears in Boston in 1819, as *The Christian Watchman.* It was published by True and Weston, Weston being a printer and becoming a believer and baptized while in charge. He was its first editor and was father of President Henry G. Weston, D.D., of Crozer Theological Seminary. Deacon James Loring was its editor for ten years or more. Rev. Ebenezer Thresher, D.D., (a notable Baptist name) was editor next in order and then came Rev. William Crowell for ten years, whose ability as a writer was widely recognized and under whom the paper took a high position. But his conservative position on questions of the day, especially slavery, antagonized many, and a paper called *The Christian Reflector* was started in Worcester, but in 1844 was removed to Boston, where under Rev. H.A. Graves it surpassed the older paper in circulation. Mr. Graves failed in health and in 1848 a consolidation of papers occurred under Rev. J.W. Olmstead and Rev. Wm. Hague. Mr. Daniel Sharp Ford, subsequently of *Youth's Companion* fame, also entered the editorial corps and by his genius made the *Watchman and Reflector* very attractive on outside and inside appearance. Steady improvement was made until in 1867 it was enlarged to an 8-page sheet with double the amount of reading matter and a slight increase of cost. Mr. Ford had large plans for the paper, but retired from the company in 1867 and entered upon his notable career with the *Youth's Companion.* The *Christian Era,* which had been started in Lowell in 1852, to express more decided anti-slavery sentiments and had good success, was merged into the *Watchman and Reflector,* the combined papers being called *The Watchman,* at the close of 1875. Doctor Olmstead had become sole editor on the retirement of Mr. Ford and continued his long and eminent career. Doctor Lorimer and Dr. Franklin Johnson were added as editors in 1876. Rev. Lucius E. Smith, D.D., took the editorial chair in 1877. In 1891, Rev. George E. Horr, D.D., became editor and brought the paper to a high standard of literary merit as a religious weekly. He changed its form from blanket sheet to the present size and shape. It was a perilous step to take, but it proved to be a stroke of wise forecast. In 1901, Rev. Edmund E. Merriam, D.D., who had had years of experience in editing and publishing the *Missionary Magazine* and literature of the American Baptist Missionary Union, was associated with Doctor Horr and succeeded him as editor-in-chief in 1904, when Doctor Horr was elected to the chair of Church History in Newton Theological Institute. At the same time Rev. Joseph S. Swaim, a pastor for 27 years, was associated with Doctor Merriam. These are still editors and largely the owners of the paper. The Watchman Publishing Company, is a stock company and has had a successful financial career and is sustained by a loyal and faithful constituency, chiefly in the New England States, although going into all the States of the Union and into Europe and Asia.

Next in order came *The Christian Secretary,* issued at Hartford, Connecticut, in 1822, under the auspices of the Connecticut Baptist Convention, but subsequently published by a corporation. In 1837, it was united with a New York paper, but this arrangement was not satisfactory and in 1838, *The Christian Secretary* was revived by its first former editor, Rev. Elisha Cushman. He was succeeded by his son until 1840. Normand Burr and others followed, but in 1861, at Mr. Burr's death, Rev. Mr. Cushman resumed editorial charge and so continued until his death in 1876, when Rev. S. Dryden Phelps, D.D., entered upon his notable service until his death. His successor, Rev. Charles A. Piddock, sold the paper to the *Examiner* of New York in 1896.

In the same year as that of the *Christian Secretary*— 1822, *The Columbian Star* was issued in Washington, D.C., by Luther Rice, assisted by Doctor Staughton. Later it was removed to Philadelphia and subsequently to Georgia, in 1833, where it is still published as *The Christian Index.* It has had notable names in its editorial ranks —Professor Knowles. Dr. Baron Stow, Dr. W.O. Brantly and Dr. H.H. Tucker. It has served the denomination in Georgia with great effectiveness. Its present editor is Dr. O.P. Bell.

In New York State, *The New York Baptist Register* was published in 1824, at Utica. This became the organ of the New York Baptist Convention and was later united with *The New York Christian Recorder,* which had grown out of the *Baptist Advocate,* with such editors as Sewall S. Cutting and Martin B. Anderson. The *United Recorder and Register* was purchased by Doctors Cutting and Edward Bright and became *The Examiner.* Upon Doctor Cutting's election to a Rochester professorship, Doctor Bright became sole editor and continued so till his death in 1894. In the first ten years he doubled its circulation and made it a power in the denomination. In 1865, *The New York Chronicle* was united with *The Examiner.* In 1867 it was enlarged to. a six-column, eight-paged paper. In 1868, *The Christian Press of* New York was united with it and in 1875 *The Outlook.* Among other names of editors of the different papers united with *The Examiner,* we find Dr. Pharcellus Church, Rev. James S. Dickerson and Rev. Henry C. Vedder, now Professor of Church History at Crozer Seminary. In 1895, *The Christian Inquirer,* Rev. John B. Calvert, D.D., editor, was consolidated with *The Examiner,* under Dr. Thomas O. Conant, and by these two as editors, *The Examiner* still ministers to the great constituency of New York State and adjacent territory.

In 1828, *Zion's Advocate* was founded by Adam Wilson, D.D., at Portland, Maine. Successive editors have been: Revs. Joseph Ricker, D.D., Lewis Colby, W.H. Shailer, D.D., H.S. Burrage, D.D., so long rendering fine service, and the present talented editor, Joseph K. Wilson, D.D. For eighty years it has had an unbroken history of service, chiefly for the people of Maine, by whom it is cherished as an old friend.

In 1831, under the auspices of the Ohio Baptist Convention, *The Baptist Weekly Journal of the Mississippi Valley,* was published at Cincinnati. Several years later a paper called *The Cross* was incorporated. Later the name was changed to *The Western Christian Journal.* Then an Indiana paper, *The Christian Messenger* was united with it and *The Journal and Messenger* appeared in 1849. Later names of editors are: Rev. J.R. Baumes, D.D., and Rev. George W. Lasher, D.D., who became sole editor in 1875, and is still at his post, vigorous and valiant, the Nestor of Baptist editors and a keen watchman of denominational and general currents of thought.

****

Baptists of Michigan had numbers and interests sufficient to demand a paper, and in 1841, *The Christian Herald* was issued in Detroit under the favoring influence of the State Convention. After some changes in the editorial chair and financial vicissitudes, it was merged into *The Christian Times and Witness* of Chicago, but was renewed by act of the Michigan Convention under the editorship of Rev. L.H. Trowbridge and wife, and as *The Christian Herald* continues as the official organ of the Convention, for the service of the Baptists of the state.

****

In 1853. the subscription list of a paper *The Watchman of the Prairies,* published at Chicago, was bought and *The Christian Times* issued. In November, 1853, Rev. Leroy Church and Rev. J.A. Smith, D.D., became proprietors and editors. Subsequently it was published by Messrs. Church and Goodman until 1875, when Dr. James. S. Dickerson, of Boston, became joint editor and sole proprietor. At his death in 1876, his widow, Emma R. Dicker- son was associated in the editorship and later his son, James Spencer Dickerson. During its 27 years it incorporated *The Illinois Baptist,* the *Witness,* of Indianapolis, and then the *Michigan Christian Herald,* when its name became *The Standard,* of Chicago. Messrs. Dickerson and R.N. VanDoren are its editors and proprietors, and issue a very able paper which covers territory far and near to

Chicago and is the leading Baptist religious weekly of the Northwest.

****

Another notable paper was *The National Baptist,* published in Philadelphia, and having editors in succession: Drs. Kendall Brooks, Lemuel Moss and H.L. Wayland. In 1894 it was incorporated in *The Examiner.*

****

Time would fail to tell of all the denominational papers started, merged and combined, but we can merely name them: The *Religious Herald,* of Richmond; the *Commonwealth,* published in Philadelphia; the *Pacific Baptist,* of California ; the *Central Baptist,* of St. Louis; the *Word and Way,* of Kansas City; the *Baptist World,* of Louisville; the *Baptist Observer,* of Indianapolis; the *Baptist Banner,* of Parkersburg, W. Va.; the *Baptist Advance,* of Little Rock, Ark.; the *Western Recorder,* of Louisville; the *Baptist Flag,* of Fulton, Ky.; the *Baptist Standard,* of Dallas, Tex.; the *Baptist Record,* of Jackson, Miss.; the *Biblical Recorder,* of Raleigh, N.C.; the *Christian Index,* of Atlanta, Ga.; the *Baptist Vanguard,* of Little Rock,. Ark.; *Baptist and Reflector,* of Nashville, Tenn.; the *Baptist Argus,* of Louisville; the *Baptist Chronicle,* of Louisiana; the *Baptist Courier,* of South Carolina; the *Baptist Observer,* of Iowa; the *Baptist Sentinel,* of Raleigh, N.C.; the *Christian Banner, of Philadelphia.* In the German list we may note: *Der Ingend Herald, Der Muntere Saeman, Der Lendbote, Der Wequeim, Der Lectiansblatter,* all of Cleveland. In the Swedish list: *Forslammungin och Hemmet, Tyrobaken, Hemmets van.*

The story of Baptist journalism shows *the projection of numerous papers under the free* and independent condition of the denomination. Rival papers have been easily started and have gained a limited reading constituency, until at length the struggle became too severe, or disaster wrecked the enterprise, and the small paper was bought by the larger one. In the more settled portions of the country the papers have now their local fields and constituency, one cannot touch on another's territory with success, and the waste and contention of two papers on one limited field have been learned as a lesson.

Our religious weeklies are highly esteemed by their subscribers and convey to them general and local information that is indispensable to their development in Christian intelligence and denominational character. The whole number of regular papers published in the United States is about seventy. In Canada the *Canadian Baptist* and the *Maritime Baptist* are published in the East, and one or two in the West. But time is not permitted to make an exhaustive review, nor to mention Baptist Journals of other countries, as England, Germany, Sweden. Our Baptist weeklies probably represent in their character and form quite fairly the intelligence and interest of their constituencies. Many have their financial difficulties, owing to the lack of full appreciation and responsibility on the part of Baptist members. But they are sustained by devoted editors and serve to guide, unify and co-ordinate the scattered hosts of the churches by whom they are held in honor and love.

THE HERALD OF GOSPEL LIBERTY
AN HISTORICAL ADDRESS
BY REV. DANIEL B. ATKINSON, A.M.[1]

It is appropriate that the centennial celebration of religious journalism should be held in the city of Portsmouth, N.H. It was here that the father of religious journalism saw the glorious vision of a free, consecrated, harmonious church. It was here that he fought the battle of personal religious freedom. It was here that he began to declare the principles of religious liberty which gave birth to the religious newspaper. It was here that he organized a company of believers into a church with the Bible as its statement of doctrine and guide in matters of discipline and with Christian as

the distinctive name for its members. It was here that the first religious newspaper was issued.

In the blessings which have flowed from the religious press, every denomination has had a large share, and so it is appropriate that we of every name and order should come here and humbly read the record of the progress and beneficent results of the religious press.

No celebration of the founding of religious journalism can be adequate and just, without some reference to the man who edited the first religious newspaper. It has often been the unhappy lot of the world's benefactors to be unappreciated by the men of their own generation, but history generally does justice to her servants. A Columbus may languish in chains, but a grateful nation will rescue his name from infamy to which prejudice would assign it, and enroll it among the immortals. The father of religious journalism is almost an unknown bene-

---

[1] Delivered in the Unitarian church on Wednesday afternoon, September 16th. Mr. Atkinson is Field Agent for the Christian College, Jireh, Wyoming.

factor of the race. His name is seldom mentioned in connection with that mighty institution for the regeneration of the world—the religious press. Your speaker would not boastfully claim that all the religious newspapers of the past century are the direct descendants of the *Herald of Gospel Liberty*, but he would be unjust to the memory of the founder of that paper if he did not claim for him the honor of making real the vision of the possible service of the religious press. In spite of ignorance, and of poverty, and of prejudice, and of calumny, he gave the world its first lesson in the value of the newspaper as a disseminator of religious intelligence. In some measure at least, we may claim for him a share in the glory of that host of stalwart penmen of the gospel who have in every denomination helped to mould the faith and direct the hands of the followers of Christ in their efforts to Christianize the world.

The world may give but little heed to what we say on this occasion, hut it cannot forget the beneficent results of the life of this pioneer of religious journalism. Men, not institutions, are the creators of new epochs. Men, not occasions and not celebrations, mark the steps of progress. We are therefore always interested in men who have figured largely in human affairs and have left to succeeding generations a legacy of blessing.

Elias Smith, the founder of religious journalism, was born of humble parentage in Lyme, Conn., June 17, 1769. When he was about thirteen years of age, his parents removed to South Woodstock, Vt. The country at that time was steep hills, buried in dense forests, with only an occasional settler's clearing. The new home was a log cabin, without roof or floor, and with a large stump standing in the middle of the one room. The whole affair was so crude that the boy rebelled and actually started to return to the old home in Connecticut.

His residence in Woodstock had an important influence upon his life. There he became inured to hardship and privation—an experience which trained him for his later years of sacrifice. There he became a school master. This marks the awakening of his keen intellect. There he had a peculiar religious experience which he afterwards recognized as his conversion. This is the beginning of his long struggle to square all his convictions by the plain teaching of the Word of God. There he had his first clear consciousness of a call to the Christian ministry, and began to prepare himself for that vocation. In 1792 he was ordained as an evangelist, carefully stipulating that he was to be free to follow the example of the apostles in traveling, and preaching the gospel. In 1802 he visited Portsmouth, and on the first day of the next January he organized a church. In this organization his independent Bible study began to bear fruit. He had been groping his way toward religious liberty. He discarded all sectarian names and professed to be merely a "Christian." He stigmatized the catechism as a human invention. In the summer of 1802, he with ten other Baptist preachers formed an organization which they called "The Christian Conference." These ministers all but committed themselves to leave behind "everything in name, doctrine, or practice, not found in the New Testament." When they saw that the logic of their position would lead them to a separation from the Baptists, they abandoned their organization. Mr. Smith, however, was not disposed to retreat, and when in 1803 he was summoned to appear before the church of Woburn to answer to charges, he immediately withdrew from the Baptists "for want of fellowship." He declared that he voluntarily joined them and that he as voluntarily withdrew from them. He stated his position in these words:

> If you wish to know what denomination I belong to I tell you as a professor of religion, I am a Christian; as a preacher, a minister of Christ; calling no man father or master; holding as abominable in the sight of God everything highly esteemed among men, such as Galvanism, Arminianism, free-willism, universalism, reverend, parsons, chaplains, doctors of divinity, clergy, bands, surplices, notes, creeds, covenants, platforms with the spirit of slander, which those who hold to these things are too often in possession of.

Notwithstanding his declaration of voluntary withdrawal, the church at Woburn excommunicated him. The church which he had organized at Portsmouth abjured all names except "Christian" and adopted the Bible as its creed and book of discipline.

Mr. Smith encountered a great deal of opposition. His enemies attacked him in print, and he began to use the same weapon. This was about 1802. His printed sermons, his "History of the Anti-Christ," "Clergyman's Looking Glass," "The Whole World Ruled by a Jew," and his pungent reviews of contemporary sermons, printed in the *Christian Magazine,* goaded on his enemies and stirred up his resourceful mind to find some new and more effective method of disseminating his religious views. While on a visit to Little Compton, R.I., in the summer of 1807, Mr. Smith met the Hon. Isaac Wilber, who made a proposal to him for the publication of a religious newspaper, which should be devoted to religious liberty. This gave Mr. Smith his cue. A newspaper—what more effective means could be used to reach the people! And Liberty! The subject that sent a thrill to his heart! But in his imagination, he heard the clanking of the slave's chains, and he remembered the persecutions which he had endured to obtain his freedom. He therefore courteously acknowledged the liberality of Mr. Wilber's proposal, but declined to accept it for the reason that he and Mr.-Wilber might not agree on what ought to be published in the paper. He had, however, imbibed the idea, and he determined to try the experiment alone. Accordingly, he set about the task and on Thursday evening, September 1, 1808, there was printed in Portsmouth, N.H., the first number of the first religious newspaper— bearing the name, "*The Herald of Gospel Liberty*," with Elias Smith as editor and publisher. It was a modest sheet, containing four pages, and was published "every other Thursday evening" at the home of the editor "near Jeffrey Street." The subscription price was one dollar per year, exclusive of postage. Fifty cents was to be paid when the first number was delivered and the other fifty when twenty-six numbers were delivered. It was to be punctually forwarded to any part of the United States where conveyance was practicable. Two hundred and seventy-four names made up the first subscription list.

Elias Smith continued to publish the *Herald of Gospel Liberty* in Portsmouth until April, 1810, when for somewhat more than a year, it was issued at Portland, Maine. Then it was moved to Philadelphia and published there until the editor returned to Portsmouth in February, 1814. In the spring of 1816, Mr. Smith moved to Boston and continued to publish his paper there until the close of 1817, when it passed into the hands of Robert Foster, who for seventeen years published it under the name of the *Christian Herald* at Portsmouth, N.H. In 1835 it was purchased by the Eastern Christian Publishing Association. Elijah Shaw was elected editor, the place of publication was changed to Exeter, N.H., and the name became the *Christian Journal.* Later the name was changed to the *Christian Herald and Journal,* and finally the word *Journal* was dropped. In 1850, the *Christian Herald* was transferred to the Christian General Book Association of Albany, N.Y., and consolidated with the *American Christian Messenger* under the name of *Christian Herald and Messenger.* The union did not prove satisfactory to the churches of New England, and one year later the Eastern Christian Publishing Association repurchased the list of *Christian Herald* subscribers and began to issue the paper independently at Newburyport, Mass., March 13, 1851, under the original name —*The Herald of Gospel Liberty.*

For years there had been some discussion of the advisability of consolidating the denominational papers. Some papers had been consolidated. The *Christian Messenger* and the *Christian Palladium* were united with the *Herald of Gospel Liberty.* All of the papers were largely localized. There was a growing demand for a publication devoted to the larger denominational interests. As a result of these discussions the *Herald of Gospel Liberty* and the *Gospel Herald* were consolidated at Dayton, Ohio, in January, 1868, under the name of the *Herald of Gospel Liberty.* It was now the property of the Christian Publishing Association, an incorporate body whose delegates at this time are the same as those of the American Christian Convention. It continues to be the property of the Association.

The *Herald of Gospel Liberty* was founded as an advocate of religious liberty. The days of Elias Smith were characterized by strong sectarian prejudices. Religious comity and fellowship were bounded by denominational lines. But there were men who saw a glorious vision of a new day, and rejoiced that the prison doors were being opened. They heard a voice saying unto them, "Stand fast therefore in the liberty wherewith Christ has made us free, and be not entangled again with the yoke of bondage." "Religious liberty," according to Elias Smith, "signifies a freedom to believe in God, and to obey Him according to the manifestation which He has made to man, in His works, in the Scriptures, and by the Spirit of truth." He regarded every kind of human law respecting religion as inconsistent with real religious liberty.

In the *Herald of Gospel Liberty* of January 19, 1810. the editor issued a "Protest," from which we give the following quotation to show the advocacy of the paper:

> I do in the first place publicly declare, that the Holy Scriptures, which contain a revelation of the will of God, are the only sure, authentic and infallible rule of the faith and practice of every Christian, by which all opinions are to be fairly and Impartially examined; and in consequence of this I do protest against setting up and allowing the decrees of any man, or body of men, as of equal authority and obligation with the word of God; whether they be councils, synods, convocations, associations, missionary societies, companies called churches, or general assemblies; whether ancient or modern, Romish, Episcopal, Presbyterian, Congregational, Baptist, or Methodist, Popes, Fathers, or Doctors of Divinity.
>
> I do further assert and maintain, according to the doctrine of Christ and the apostles, and the practice of Christians in the first century ; that in all things essential to the faith and practice of a Christian, the Scriptures are plain, and easy to be understood, by all who will diligently and Impartially read and study them ; and that charging the Scriptures with obscurity and uncertainty is contrary to the plain declaration of the Scriptures, and is an abuse of the rule given for Christians to walk by, and an insult upon the Holy Spirit by which the authors of them were guided.
>
> I do further assert that every Christian is under an indispensable obligation to search the Scripture for himself, and make the best use of it he can for his information in the will of God, and the nature of pure religion; that he hath an unalienable right, Impartially to judge the sense and

meaning of it, and to follow the Scripture wherever it leads him, even an equal right with the bishops and pastors of the churches; and in consequence of this I further protest against that unrighteous and ungodly pretense of making writings of the fathers, the decrees of councils and synods, or the sense of the church, the rule and standard of judging the sense of the Scriptures as popish. anti-Christian, and dangerous to the church of God,

I do further assert and maintain that every Christian hath an equal right to the peaceable and constant possession of what he believes to be the truth contained in the Scriptures, and ought to be left by all men, and secured by the civil government, in the full and undisturbed enjoyment of them; even though his principles may in many things be contrary to what the Reverend D.D.'s call Orthodoxy.

As truth is no man's private property, and all Christians, are under obligations to propagate it; I do also declare that every Christian has a right to publish and vindicate what he believes is contained in the Scriptures; to speak and to write against all corruption of the word, either in doctrine or practice; and to expose the errors of good men, and the wickedness, oppression and hypocrisy of ungodly men ; that every Christian has not only a right, but is commanded to separate from such professors whose doctrine and worship are contrary to what he finds recorded in the Scriptures ; and that he has a right to enjoy without disturbance, oppression or disgrace or any kind of punishment, civil or ecclesiastical, the liberty of serving God, with any other company of Christians, as he shall judge most expedient and useful to him.

In 1816, when Mr. Smith's work as editor of the *Herald of Gospel Liberty* was practically completed, he defined his position as follows:

The Holy Scriptures are the only sure, authentic and infallible rule of faith and practice; the name Christian is the only proper one for the believer; in all essentials the

Scriptures are plain to be understood; every Christian is free to examine the Scriptures for himself and to impartially judge the sense and meaning of the same; every Christian has a right to publish and vindicate what he believes is contained in the Scriptures and to serve God according to his own conscience.

The principles of religious liberty as advocated by Elias Smith at the beginning of his journalistic career were but little altered at any time by him, and governed the conduct of the paper under his editorial management. He contended earnestly for the Word of God as the final source of appeal in religious matters. He opposed doctrines and dogmas which could not be stated in the language of the Bible. He was relentless in his opposition to religious despotism and his paper teemed with articles on liberty. His bitter invectives were hurled relentlessly against church polities, clerical trappings, ministerial titles, ecclesiastical associations, hireling preachers, creeds and all the "isms" which to him seemed to be forms of religious tyranny. He contended for apostolic simplicity in church organizations and in religious worship.

The *Herald of Gospel Liberty* however, was more than an arena for the discussion of theological questions. It was in a true sense a religious newspaper. On the first page of each number of the early volumes these words were printed as the motto of the paper:

> From realms far distant, and from climes unknown; we make the knowledge of our King your own.

The purpose of the paper was expressed in the following poem which appeared in the first number,

> *Had I a thousand mouths, a thousand tongues,*
> *A throat of brass and adamantine lungs,*
> *I'd sound redeeming love through all the earth,*
> *The love that gave me first and second birth;*
>
> *I'd tell to all creation's utmost space,*
> *How great His goodness and how rich His grace*

Till wondering nations should His grace adore,
Jehovah's Christ, God blest for ever more.

One of the most important departments was called "Religious Intelligence." In this department appears reports from churches, ministers, and conferences or general gatherings. It was through the *Herald of Gospel Liberty* that the Christians of New England, the South and the West became acquainted and were gradually drawn into a closer fellowship. In 1812 there was but one state in the Union where the paper was not sent.

In 1818 Robert Foster had secured control of the paper and sent forth his first number from Portsmouth in May, bearing the name *Christian Herald.* The character of the paper was greatly changed "by the new editor.

"Perhaps the time has come," the editor wrote, "when arguments instead of censure, and entreaties instead of the scourge may do more for the cause of truth than a host of censurers and volumes of invectives."

It was proposed to give particular attention to the manners and customs of the times in which the Scriptures were written, to present such historical subjects and miscellaneous articles as would be consistent with the design of the paper, to give accounts of the revivals of religion among the denominations, to present foreign religious information and to make the paper the herald of the pleasing intelligence that Christians of every denomination were manifesting a larger liberty and a warmer fellowship which were prophetic of the coming day when they would all be one.

The controversial spirit disappears almost completely, and the *Christian Herald* was indeed the harbinger of a more peaceful day.

For seventeen years Robert Foster carried the burden of this publication. He was both editor and publisher. His financial resources drained and his health destroyed, he surrendered his papers to the Eastern Christian Publishing Association, and Elijah Shaw became the editor. The *Christian Herald* became the *Christian Journal.*

April 1835, marks a decided change in the history of this paper. Before that time, it had been the property of individuals and had a hard struggle to maintain its existence. It then passed into the control of an association. The whole character of the paper was changed so as to meet the needs of the growing denomination. The three independent movements out of which came the Christian Connection, had merged into one, and churches had been established in Canada and in nearly every state east of the Mississippi. The churches had been organized into conferences, and the conferences were working together through a General Convention, now known as the American Christian Convention.

The *Christian Journal* was responsive to this enlarging denominational life. The paper was enlarged, and was issued semi-monthly until 1839. Since that time, it has been published weekly. The number of contributors was greatly increased. The departments of the paper were changed, and included contributed articles, editorials, religious intelligence, obituaries, youth's department, temperance, and notices. The motto of the paper was expressed in these words: "In necessary things, unity; in non-essentials, liberty; in all things, charity."

It will be impossible to give a detailed review of the *Herald of Gospel Liberty* under the management of each of its editors. We shall therefore be content with some brief references to the advocacy of the paper concerning some of the vital subjects of discussion.

From 1835 to the close of the Civil War, slavery was a living issue in politics and in religion. In 1838 the Association passed a resolution providing that the columns of the *Christian Journal* should be open for articles on the evils and sin of slavery, so far as the same may involve the fundamental principles of morality and religion. Three years previous some articles had appeared on this subject. The first one began with these words: "We believe slavery to be sin, always, everywhere, and only sin." These words express the attitude of the paper towards the institution of slavery. As the years passed and the war- clouds began to gather, the opposition became more intense. Doubtless the strong denunciation of slavery by the Various contributors and editors had much to do in paving the way for the unfortunate division in the General Convention at Cincinnati, when the southern delegates withdrew and the southern churches formed an independent body. When the war came and

President Lincoln issued his call for volunteers to defend the Union, the *Herald of Gospel Liberty* gave the full measure of its influence to the Union cause, urged the citizens of the Republic to enlist in the national army, and advocated the overthrow of the institution of slavery. When the war was over and the citizens of our great Republic were again devoting their energies to the arts of peace, the *Herald of Gospel Liberty* preached the gospel of peace and good will. It contributed its share towards the consummation of the union of the churches North and South—a union which is an accomplished fact, and today in the Christian denomination there is no North, no South, for we are all brethren.

The Herald of Gospel Liberty has been patriotic, an advocate of justice, a defender of the oppressed, an enemy of corruption, a foe of the liquor traffic, a friend of man.

On the subject of education, the paper has not been uniform in its attitude. Its first editor lived in troublous days. He was much persecuted for his faith, and his life was always a strenuous one. Some of his positions were certainly unsound. This is especially true of his attitude toward education. He emphasized strongly the necessity of a call to the ministry, and evidently thought that a college man could only be a man-made minister. It is not strange then that the *Herald* under his management should be opposed to an educational qualification for the minister. After the days of Elias Smith, the opposition to a literary education gradually ceased but it was not until the days of Elijah Shaw, Daniel P. Pike and Austin Craig that the *Herald* became the friend and defender of the theological seminary. Under the influence of these men, many friends of education were raised up, and nearly all the movements which have resulted in the founding of church schools have been greatly accelerated by the co-operation of the *Herald*. Starkey Seminary, the Christian Biblical Institute, Antioch College, arid Union Christian College especially found a warm supporter in our church paper, and in recent years the *Herald* has had a department devoted to the interests of education.

The early ministers of the Christian Church were nearly all missionaries. Abner Jones, Elias Smith, Mark Fernald, Elijah Shaw, Barton W. Stone, David Purviance, James O'Kelly, and a host of others travelled extensively and preached the gospel wherever they found an open door. These men and their successors gave character to the *Herald of Gospel Liberty*, and made it the preacher of a missionary gospel. Under Robert Foster news from the foreign land was gladly welcomed. If the denomination was slow in sending its missionaries to the heathen, we can still truthfully say that the pioneer of religious journalism long and earnestly advocated the work in foreign lands, and when a leader was found to direct the missionary zeal in practical channels, the *Herald* was the medium through which our beloved Dr. J.P. Watson reached the members of the church and interested them in his children's mission, from which have evolved our present missionary enterprises. The missionary department of the paper had been wisely and faithfully used to foster Christian work at home and abroad.

Time fails me in which to speak of the splendid work of the *Herald of Gospel Liberty* in the interest of temperance, the home, the Sunday-school, the Young People's Society, the American Christian Convention, and a host of other denominational enterprises.

The *Herald* has been fortunate in its editors and contributors. Elias Smith, its founder and first editor, was a natural, forceful orator, a successful evangelist, an able sermonizer, an intrepid reformer, a brilliant journalist. His character was above reproach. His conscience was tender. His love of liberty was deep and abiding. By temperament, by zeal, by a wide experience, he was well fitted to be the leader of a new movement. While his habit of introspection sometimes caused him to be despondent and his reformatory zeal occasionally led him astray, yet his doctrinal contentions largely foreshadowed the accepted position of the church today. His positions on the education and support of the ministry, and the organization of churches and conferences were probably unsound, still his note of warning was not wholly unjustified by prevailing conditions. "On the whole he was a remarkable man, and lacked little of true greatness, being one of the commanding figures of his day in New England."

His successor in the editorial chair was a man of a different type. Robert Foster was not a preacher. He was a man of kind and gentle disposition. He loved the church and was enraptured with the service of his Master. When Elias Smith lost his standing with the Christian Connection because of his acceptance of Universalism, the confidence of the church in the *Herald of Gospel Liberty* was shaken. Robert Foster was the man to restore that confidence. He was neither narrow nor bigoted in his denominational views, but no one ever charged him with disloyalty. He successfully piloted his enterprise through the troubled waters, until he gave his charge into the hands of his successor, the Rev. Elijah Shaw.

Elijah Shaw was a man of versatile talents. A careful student, an interesting preacher, a splendid organizer, a prodigious worker, he made his paper a voice of authority, calling for renewed vigor in evangelistic, educational, temperance, benevolent and missionary enterprises. Under the inspiration of his pen, New England took on new life. He was largely instrumental in saving the churches from the delusion of Millerism, and in checking the advances of Campbellism.

For one year the *Herald* was united with the *Christian Messenger* of Albany, N.Y., with the Rev. Jasper Hazen as editor, and then it returned to New England. This was in 1851. For a number of years then there was an editorial board composed of Daniel P. Pike, John B. Weston, O.J. Wait, E. Edmunds, David E. Millard, Austin Craig, Thomas Holmes, John W. Haley, B.F. Summerbell and others. These names are the guarantee of the excellent character of the paper. Daniel P. Pike was the stalwart defender of the principles of the Christian Church. John B. Weston for years has stood for the education of our ministers, and no history of our educational work would be complete without the mention of his name. Austin Craig was the prophet of the Christian Biblical Institute, the peerless teacher of Biblical theology. Thomas Holmes is our classical theologian and educator.

For some years previous to 1863 Benjamin F. Carter was the resident editor of the *Herald* with John W. Haley associate editor.

In 1868 the Rev. Henry Y. Rush became editor. Doctor Rush was a forceful writer, a clear thinker, a thoughtful friend, and under him the *Herald* became the organ of the Christian Church, and the preacher of a pure gospel. His voice was the voice of inspiration.

He was followed by the historian of our church, Dr. N. Summerbell. Doctor Summerbell had deep convictions, and an intense love for the truth. He was a ready writer and speaker. He believed that our cause is the cause of heaven and we have no right to resign it, betray it, forsake or neglect it.

His successor was the advocate of temperance and "loving religion," the Rev. Dr. Thomas M. McWhinney, who in later years has made a reputation for himself as an author and lecturer.

The Rev. Asa W. Coan and the Rev. C.J. Jones, D.D. were forceful orators, as well as clear and vigorous writers. The Rev. Mr. Coan was disqualified for his duties by a stroke of paralysis, and Doctor Jones was called into the evangelistic field—a work for which he was well qualified. His successor was the Rev. Dr. Josiah P. Watson, whose recent departure brought sadness to the hearts of the entire brotherhood. He was much loved by all the people, for he was the friend of all. A man of large sympathies, of intense loyalty and capable of prodigious tasks, he identified himself with the whole denominational life.

For about eight months in 1893 the Rev. George D. Black wielded a versatile pen in the editorial office as an associate editor with Doctor Watson.

Of the two remaining editors, the Rev. J.J. Summerbell, D.D., and the present incumbent, the Rev. J. Pressley Barrett, D.D., I forbear to speak, except to say that the present modern, vigorous, loyal, spiritual *Herald of Gospel Liberty* owes its many recent improvements in character and mechanical make-up to their strong, judicious editorial work.

It remains only for me to say a few words concerning the spirit of the *Herald of Gospel Liberty*.

If we go back a hundred years, we shall find ourselves in a different world. It was a world of controversy. One writer describes it as follows:

> On every side the voice of controversy was blatant. Arminianism accused Calvinism, Adult-baptism smote Pedo-baptism, Predestinarianism belabored Freedom of the Will, Free Grace trampled upon Election. Every pulpit was an entrenched redoubt from safe spot to deliver hot shot,

well aimed, not so much against sin and sinners as against the pulpit across the way. What the ministers expounded the deacons and the people elaborated. Theological debate was rife, in the parlor, in the kitchen, in the tavern and in the blacksmith shop. Church members, or unregenerate persons, all had the language of dogmatic contention, and all were naming their adversaries reproachfully, and consigning them to the nethermost perdition. To complete the picture of the period, one must remember that on the frontier line there was no lack of primitive vices. Brawling, Sabbath-breaking, profane cursing, drunkenness and profligacy were so common that the letters of the period, as well as the sermons that have come down to us, all have their wail at the prevalence of iniquity.

"Into a society like this, of sinners sinning exceedingly, and of saints quarrelling contumaciously" came the *Herald of Gospel Liberty*, "declaring the sinfulness of sin, and proclaiming everywhere that men should repent, and that Christians without respect to their opinions should serve the same Christ, and live together in brotherly fellowship." The central idea in the *Herald of Gospel Liberty* has been the Christ, and the contention of the editors and contributors has been for the right of the individual to come into personal fellowship with Him. That was the meaning of its supporters when they wrote in its platform the declaration that the Bible is the only creed of the church, the Christ is the only head of the church, and the name Christian is the proper distinctive designation of the follower of the Master.

They reasoned in this fashion: God has spoken to men. A portion of that message has been crystallized into the Bible. What has been written is for our instruction, and is the final source of appeal in all matters of doubt or discussion. The adoption of any doctrinal statement as fundamental in church government is to dethrone the Bible and to deny to the individual the right of personal investigation. If they opposed creeds and doctrines and forms of church government—and they did oppose these things— it was because they believed these things stood as barriers between the believer and his Christ.

They wished to be a Bible people, and their theology to be Biblical theology. For that reason, they contended that doctrines should be expressed in the language of the Bible. Their love for the Christ inspired them to place great emphasis upon His leadership. He is the head of the church. They adopted the name Christian, not because they denied that others were Christians, but as most suggestive and promotive of Christian fellowship.

It seems not to have occurred to the early writers that there could be any serious differences of opinion among free Christians. Time however revealed to them the fact that not all their differences were removed by the freedom granted their members. Two important questions were therefore raised: (1.) What are the rights of the individual in such cases? (2.) What shall be the basis of fellowship?

The first question was answered by the editor when he asserted that every Christian is under an indispensable obligation to search the Scriptures for himself, and to publish and vindicate what he believes is contained therein.

As to the basis of fellowship, it was declared that not dogma but vital piety, not belief concerning the Christ, but ' attitude toward Him, not theological opinion, but Christian character should be the determining factor. If a man by his life shows the fruits of the Spirit, he should be fellowshipped as a Christian.

And so, the spirit of the *Herald of Gospel Liberty* has been one of loyalty to God, to His Son, Jesus Christ, and to His Word, the Holy Scriptures. The liberty of the Christian is bounded on all sides by the sphere in which God reigns, and within that sphere he is to be untrammeled, by the traditions of the fathers.

OTHER DENOMINATIONAL PUBLICATIONS
BY PROF.J.N. DALES[1]

It was probably the purpose of the committee in assigning this subject to me that some representation might be granted to the first heathen (?) country which the Christians attempted to evangelize. We often speak of Japan as being our first foreign mission field. It is at least a debatable question whether this may not be an historical inaccuracy since the Canadian Foreign Mission Enterprise was inaugurated spontaneously by ministers from New York State over seventy years ago and has been untouched by all such tragedies as mission treasury deficits.

Outside of our greatest enterprise, that of publishing for one hundred years the *Herald of Gospel Liberty*, we have made some contributions which may fairly be considered of substantial value to religious literature.

In the southland *The Christian Sun* has been published more than sixty years and there may be some present today who will have the pleasure of witnessing its centennial, for verily its natural force is not abated and its vision is keener and its enterprise more aggressive than ever. It is a doughty champion of the right and a loyal and trusted representative of the Christian Church, south.

The Christian Vanguard of Ontario is now reaching up to manhood, has an increasing number of loyal supporters, aims at representing the Canadian church which owns and controls it and is proud to number itself among the religious forces which the Christians are trying to direct in order to enthrone righteousness in this North America of ours and the world at large.

[1] Delivered on Wednesday afternoon, September 16, in Unitarian Church. Mr. Dales is Professor of French McMaster University, Toronto, Canada.

Like all other movements our new Protestantism has had its aggressive leaders and champions and today their names are household words in our homes. It would be strange indeed were not some records of the lives of these men left to us in books. Here and there an enthusiastic admirer, or a convert, has seized the pen and given us word pictures of the old strenuous days when verily it seemed to be the purpose of all men "to contend for the faith." We have not one too many of these books. The lives of Shaw, Walter, Summerbell, Craig, Millard, Gardner, and a host of others inspire us to live a life that is worth while. They teach us, too, that men with strong convictions regarding life and doctrine are certain to be purposeful, persistent and successful in evangelistic and pastoral work. The Standing Committee on Publications will do well to encourage this feature of our literary output.

In ethics and philosophy our Publishing House has issued interesting and suggestive works from the pen of Dr. T.M. McWhinney, whose recent literary effort entitled, *The Democracy of Religion* has been most favorably received by the press.

At the January, (1908) meeting of the Publication Committee, it was decided to accept for publication and circulation the manuscript of a story entitled *A Puritan Captain.* This is a radical departure in policy. It is believed, however, that the business and privilege of a publishing association is to send forth any book whose purpose is healthy and heartening. The committee believe, therefore, that they have pursued the right course.

We have issued tracts in abundance and at present thousands of these leave our House every year. They deal with evangelistic interests, discuss doctrinal subjects and forward missionary and denominational plans.

As a body of religious workers, we have always laid stress upon the vital doctrines of Christianity. (See *Scripture Doctrine,* Dr. J.J. Summerbell, Dr. J.B. Weston, and others.)

Our creed is the Bible, we aim to express Bible truths in Bible language, and we long for the time when all denominations will be known only as Christians, thus emphasizing that "name which is above every name."

The interests of church union have found frequent and forceful expression in our literature. This is a consummation devoutly to be wished, but, if it is to be lasting, we see how inevitable and spontaneous must be the causes promoting it. We, therefore, accept and strive to further this movement by whatever plans Christian fellowship suggests, having always due regard for that which has been committed to our care.

Our Sunday-school literature is one of the most important departments of our work, as a publishing association. Its circulation has now reached unprecedented figures and the opportunity of the Sunday-school editor, as he speaks from week to week to his vast audience of adults and children, is a privilege justly prized and nobly used both by our dear departed Doctor Watson and his faithful successor.

Besides numerous local papers, we have yet to mention *The Christian Missionary* and Dr. J.G. Bishop, the man whose claims upon our gratitude have never yet been entirely understood, nor fully appreciated. He has built something that has endured—a sure proof of his forethought and wise management.

And now a word in conclusion, even should it seem visionary. Why not a *Christian Culture Course* for our young people—our Christian Endeavorers, and our sometime licentiates and ministers.

The lives of the founders of our movement afford rich material for such study. Their problems are our problems and their vigorous faith and purposeful lives are well calculated to inspire us for the battle of life.

NORTH CONGREGATIONAL CHURCH
Where Wednesday Evening Session was held.

91

THE EDUCATIONAL INFLUENCE OF RELIGIOUS JOURNALISM

BY REV. MARTYN SUMMERBELL, D.D.[1]

Barely a hundred years ago, —but such a hundred, crowded with great events, more than could be expressed in a Cycle of Cathay, Elias Smith ventured in this old New Hampshire town of Portsmouth, to edit and publish the *Herald of Gospel Liberty*, the first religious journal in the world. It was a step into an unknown field, an enterprise as daring in its way as Columbus' voyage from Palos, or the landing of the Pilgrims on Plymouth Rock; counting

not merely the one periodical, but the multitude of which it was the harbinger, and carrying results hardly less momentous and far-reaching. In that little sheet, facsimiles of which many of you possess, as in the pent-up gases of Jovite or Shimose, lay the power to shake a nation to its moral center and overwhelm the frowning citadel of sin.

That journalism, speaking in the broadest way, is an educational force requires no discussion. Of course, it is understood that many of the sheets that are ground out in such daily profusion, are not possessed of the loftiest ideals. It is a matter of common knowledge that some publications are chiefly concerned to sell so many miles of white paper, and worry themselves little over what is impressed on the paper. Be it what it may:—the story of how the dirt flies at Panama, or the latest racy domestic Intelligence from Sioux Falls; the synopsis of Dr. Eloquent's latest top-loftical sermon or the explanation of how the three-card monte man swindles the rubes; the half-tone of the tallest Manhattan skyscraper or the colored page,

[1] Delivered on Wednesday evening, September 16th, in the North Congregational church. Dr. Summerbell is President of Palmer Institute-Starkey Seminary, Lakemont, N.Y.

showing Buster Brown in his cheerful arrangement of a bent pin for the elevation of Grandpa Brown:—all is grain for his grist and fish for his net, so long as it helps sell the paper. And it is equally a matter of common knowledge that some pens are venal, and are to be bought and sold with the plant, so that within twenty-four hours the same hand may have been advocating high-tariff or no tariff; free gambling or antigambling. Yet, for all that, the press as a whole, clean papers or yellow papers; papers that print all the news that it is fit to print, or papers in which, if you see it, you know that it is so, or papers that you hardly want to pick up with the tongs; — papers, good, bad or indifferent; — all are helping to mold life and teach the people. You know that they have a saying over in England that the ha'penny press is educating the world, and there is no little truth in the suggestion. As a matter of fact, I am far less keen than I used to be in my antagonism to certain periodicals. At one time I was strongly of the notion that what America wanted was a censor of the press, empowered like the censor in Russia to blot out objectionable copy from any publication. But with my present experience of life, I have come to see that the ruder mind must have its ruder portraiture, and that it is far better for the untrained, or the half-trained to read something, rather than to be scared by the high-toned propriety of our first-class periodicals into reading nothing at all. It was a wise speech of Dr. Johnson's when he said: "Read anything five hours a day and you will become learned," and the thought has this application to the press, that reading almost anything is better than no reading, and that no editor or publisher can put out a sheet which the American public will buy, that can be altogether bad, or that will not present something to awaken intelligence and broaden the understanding. Even the absurdities of the professional crank will stir the reader to resent his foolishness, and the vicious sneer of the hireling against truth, and purity, and goodness rouses up a spirit that sees truth and purity and goodness in clearer perspective, and so teaches to admire the admirable. Certainly, the press is an educational power, as every man knows who recalls how the *London Times,* the Thunderer, used to make and unmake Prime Ministers, or how Missouri Border Ruffians hated Owen Lovejoy's paper, or how Horace Greeley's *Tribune* wakened the North to sustain the Union, or how Thomas Nast's caustic pencil helped Father Knickerbocker to turn the rascals out of the House of Plunder. The same power is exercised no less today. Charles E. Hughes is a great man, but the people would not yet have discovered his greatness, bad not the press printed his masterly investigations and scattered broadcast his manly appeals and addresses. The Roman poet Vergil once pictured dead souls in the nether world as suspended from trees, where their evil taint was beaten out by rain and wind; and so today measures and men are suspended before the American people on the columns of the press, their evil exposed to the wholesome scorn of a clean-souled citizenship.

It is because of the power of the press that great business concerns are operating the "square deal," and that with the politicians, graft, the shaking of the plum tree, and addition, division and silence are going out of date, until we have come to that pass in our national life that only men of clean record dare aspire to high office, and that now, as we are on the threshold of a presidential election we can be assured that we have clean men for our leaders; men so clean, and pure, and noble that no man—broadminded man, or rankest partisan—dare lift a railing accusation against them. That way it was not one hundred years ago, nor fifty, nor twenty. The vituperations hurled at a political opponent in the days of Washington, of Jefferson, of Jackson, of Lincoln, of Blaine, were a disgrace to the nation, and force us to hide our faces in shame, did we not know that the most of them were manufactured for the occasion, and that those who circulated them the most briskly believed them only till the vote was cast. As a fact, statesmen and statesmanship have been growing in character. Personal conduct is on the higher plane than when General Washington had to rebuke Charles Lee on Monmouth field, and when in the forties and fifties a political banquet wound up with half of the guests under the table. The American patriot has been educated to better ways and much of the change is doubtless due to the intelligence, the activity and the growing sense of honor of the American press.

Much of what has just been said will apply with justice to the religious press. I say much, but by no means all; for religious journalism has its own field, in which it owns opportunities and exerts activities which are peculiarly its own. When we come to observe this field and the activities mentioned, we observe that both are wide. For religious journalism begins with the child, just able to toddle to the infant class of the Sunday-school, and it follows his whole career, taking it for granted that he inclines to religious sympathy, so long as he has an eye to read, or a mind to comprehend.

Every time that a child reaches out his hand for the Sunday-school paper; every time the man, seated at his fireside opens up his *Herald of Gospel Liberty,* his *Advocate,* his *Observer,* his *Morning Star,* his *Independent,* his *Outlook,* his *Advance;* every time the minister in his study peruses his denominational quarterly; every time the mission class reads from the *Endeavor World,* or the *Mission Monthly,* he is under the educational influence of religious journalism. Because it enjoys the freedom of the home circle, because it touches the profoundest emotions of the human heart, faith, hope, duty, love; because it plays skillfully and persistently on these emotions all the way from the cradle to the grave, we recognize that its educational influence must be potent and abiding.

The aim of religious journalism brings us to the same conclusion. All of its purposes are educative, and *all the* more so, since they are exercised in so many forms, and touch the reader on so many sides of his being.

The religious journal educates because it disseminates religious intelligence. Back a century ago the new journalism must have been narrow, and every one of the denominational organs, as each came into being, made it its business to give out the news of its own body, with very slight concern for the others, unless the mention made of the others was uncomplimentary. Today, religious journalism is on a broader plane. It is so, because all our life is broader, and we see that whatever affects others religiously has presently effects upon ourselves. Accordingly, all wide-awake religious journals, whether denominational, or interdenominational, report all occurrences that generally affect the religious world. Any movement of importance, whether the planting of a new mission station on the other side of the world, or the starting of settlement work in the slums of a great city, or the call of the governor of a great commonwealth for the people to rally to his support as he pushes some fresh phase of moral reform, is spread out its pages, and so it is brought at once to the hearts of the people who are most interested in that class of intelligence. May it be said that the purveying of news is the business of the secular press, and that it will be well attended to by that agency, without need of help from the religious press? That may be so to a degree, but to a degree only, for the agency is so uncertain. The secular press to its credit has discovered that there is good money in some kinds of religious news. We remember how a great newspaper telegraphed the entire Revised New Testament from New York to Chicago, and printed it for its readers, while express trains were carrying the printed books that bad come over from Oxford, across the continent. But it has to be remembered that the secular press in sizing up the value of religious news has its own standard. It figures all the news by commercial rating. It wants most that kind of news that goes with a two- or three-inch scare head. Accordingly, the secular press purveys the religious news, which is rarely of the scare-head sort, sporadically and incompletely. Time and again you will see, even in your favorite daily, an entire broadside given up to the account of a murder case, or a divorce case, or a prize fight, while a great religious convention will get merely an obscure corner. If an elephant breaks away from a circus and makes a ten-mile run across country, he will have a column, telling graphically how he burst through the excited crowd, how the women went into hysterics, bow be lifted a horse over a fence, and how at last he was corralled in Farmer X's barnyard and subdued by a pack of men with pitchforks. But the same paper will cut the death and career of a prominent divinc, who has devoted his life to the service of God and the church, to ten or twenty lines. In this manner the secular press presents a distorted picture in the album of life. It exalts the sensational and minimizes the important.

To restore tone and reality to the picture, is the province of the religious press. It must hold the true balance. It must display the religious intelligence which the secular press has reported half-way, or suppressed. To know what is really happening in the religious world—to have the facts of religious happenings and tendencies displayed before the mind, so that it may have reliable material for thought, is educational, and wisely educational.

The religious journal educates also because it gives sane and adequate discussion of religious questions. Here again we may be advised that the secular press is emulating the religious press, and that it is laying hold of great questions in an intelligent manner. And we will readily grant the proposition to a limited degree. The great reviews and the dailies of our largest cities will frequently give considerable space to religious themes that happen to be prominent in the public mind. But here again we observe the same discrimination that we noted before. For the secular press to take up this sort of copy, there must be in it something of the sensational already, and then the secular editors will toss oil on the sensational blaze to make it flash up more sensationally. Very seldom does the secular press drag out a neglected religious topic with the purpose of teaching the people a better understanding of the fundamentals of life. But the religious journal is established to make religious truths vital in the hearts of the people. Here is the broad field of religious truth, the fundamental things, right philosophies of being, an intelligent view of the Creator, and man's relation to the infinite and the future, the entire range of human duty, and the boundless perspectives of human destiny—all these wonderfully important topics are continually under earnest discussion in the religious press. In bringing such themes prominently and persistently before the people, and in familiarizing them with the ripest thought of the age respecting them, the religious press is accomplishing a far-reaching educational work.

Another important function of religious journalism is that of impressing religious obligation. While the religious paper sets the people to thinking, it is also pointing out cogently how the right thinking should materialize into the form of right doing. It calls to mind the various benevolences of the church and urges the reader to give them moral and material support. It prints the appeals of the denominational secretaries, and frequently indicates ways and means for rousing the people to more generous contributions. A familiar example of this phase of religious journalism was seen in the last Chinese famine. Then the religious press of the English-speaking world, — for it is where English is spoken that the religious press is most flourishing, —wrote up the situation of the suffering thousands, and gave pictorial representations of households in all stages of destitution and starvation, and offered their services free of charge for the forwarding of gifts and supplies for the alleviation of a nation's wretchedness. Similarly, in a recent wave of temperance reform that has been sweeping state after state in the Southland, it was the co-operation of the religious press, with the pulpit and the secular press that brought to home after home a serious conviction of the evil of the open saloon, and enlisted preacher, and deacon, and business man, and laboring man, and mothers, and sisters, and daughters to declare that the saloon must go.

Please to observe that I am not claiming that the religious press accomplished it all, but I do contend that it was a prominent factor in the contest, and that in default of its aid, the work would have been far less effective and extensive.

Further, we are not to lose sight of the fact that the educational influence of religious journalism is the stronger, from the methods it pursues, and which in their present perfection it was long time in working out.

The religious press has educational influence all the greater because it has borrowed from the secular press the art of making itself attractive. In form, in dress, by which we mean the style of type which is artistic and satisfying to the eye, in lavish use of the pictorial illustration, it is making all the time a silent appeal to be read. I take up the first issue of the *Herald of Gospel Liberty*, and I find it a creditable piece of workmanship for that period. Its type was readable, its page was well proportioned, and its general makeup, as compared with contemporary secular Issues, quite up to the mark. But the *Herald of Gospel Liberty* of today is larger of course, and it has better type, and it enjoys the benefit of present-day methods of Illustrative display. As they lie side by side on your table with the secular papers and magazines of the time, the religious journals of 1908 invite perusal with promise that the reader's time will not be spent in vain.

The religious journal has educational influence from the fact that it has learned to treat interesting things interestingly. Carlyle used to maintain that the average German historian, whom he nick-named Dr. Dry-as-Dust, was the driest sort of writer on the face of the earth. A great deal of religious writing has been framed on that model. But our best religious papers cannot be accused of that fault. They choose fresh topics; they handle them interestingly and they polish them with that literary touch which pleases any class of mind. They cover all departments of religious life. They give you a Sunday-school department for the children, and an Endeavor de-partment for the young people, all kinds of departments for the general church work, and the general pages for everybody. Meet-ing thus all sorts of mind, with material that is fitted for each and all, they are touching the people far more than we commonly take account of.

In this review we are also not to lose sight of the popular tone that the religious press has adopted. In all its presentations, news, narratives, editorial discussions or beneficiary appeals, it comes down to the vernacular, and employs terms that are current today. Teachers have a maxim that they must teach at the level of the pupil's intelligence. The wise teacher has to be in advance of his student, for if he lags, the pupil loses ground; but he must be not too far afield, else the pupil is lost and is at standstill. I have known some preachers to fly so high above the heads of the people as to miss them altogether; and other preaching that was too trivial, ex-plaining laboriously what the people knew well enough already. Journalism might show the like error.

We have special publications that are intended for special classes of readers, and they are about as intelligible to the average man as so much Greek, or Choctaw. On my desk I have regularly the *Medico-Legal Journal.* Lawyers can read it. Physicians can read it. College men can read it. But to the general public a clay tablet from Nineveh would convey just about as much information. On my desk is another publication, a popular magazine, and in it a distinguished divine explains the course of copying, to which the Bible has been subjected since the fourth century. In the space of ten lines, he uses terms like these: "Gone the way of all papyri;" "gone the way of all flesh;" "heir of all those ages;" "the Hebrew amanuensis." The passage was brilliant, and the content was perfectly intelligible to those for whom it was intelligible. But what will the general public make out of it? Now it is to the advantage of the religious press that when it sets out to talk to the people, it uses the language of the people. It speaks directly to the home, cutting out pomposity on the one hand and frivolity on the other, and so the people read, understand and are instructed.

A further advantage of the religious press in its aim of education, is that of periodicity. Whatever it sets out to impress it can present today, next week, and the next week again—not by any means in the same form, for that would make it flat, stale and unprofitable, —but first in one light and then in another, until it is made the reader's own possession. Long ago the evangelical prophet set forth that fundamental maxim of pedagogy: "precept must be upon precept, precept upon precept; line upon line, line upon line; here a little and there a little." So modern educators are insisting on the same principle when they declare the importance of graving on the material substance of the brain, until the picture becomes so distinct and permanent that no subsequent experiences, however striking, can wash it away. It is thus that the religious journal travels on its spiritual mission week after week, bearing its messages to the people. It has a place that cannot be taken by any other agency. Count up your educational forces, your pulpits, your Bible schools, your secular schools from the lowest to the highest, your daily press to which I have already accorded a high place in popular training, but ever leave large room for the religious press, for which I claim nothing less than its due, when I call it the university for the people. In its columns are Instruction and stimulus for every mind. The child who attends the school, and the adult, whose school-days are all over, scans its pages and learns continually new lessons of fact, of philosophy, of progress, from its every issue.

Tell me that the religious press is stupid, and that subscribers have to be cudgeled into its support. In general, such allegation has no foundation. There are dull religious papers, precisely as there are some prosy preachers, and some moss-backed lawyers, and some stupid teachers; but exactly as the mass of preachers, lawyers and teachers are wide-awake and live to the present age, so I may say for the mass of religious papers that they are attractive and influential. I can name you religious papers by dozen that are welcomed in the household; that are by fathers, mothers and children, and read even more intently than the daily newspaper. I know such religious papers about which there is a friendly rivalry in the family, as to who shall get the first reading; which are no sooner let fall by one than they are picked up by another, and read diligently from the first page to the last.

A journal that so captures the people is a living force, and its power to mold thought and life is incalculable.

Subject, if you please, what I am saying to a few simple tests.

Where will you find the best understanding of, and the most appreciative reception of, religious instruction? Will it not be from fatherhood, motherhood and childhood, from homes where the competent religious journal is taken and read most faithfully?

When you attempt to secure contributions for missionary or other benevolent purposes, will you not get the most relatively, that is, in proportion to the means of the givers, from the homes that support the religious journal, and which consequently, are the best informed as to the needs of the cause you represent?

Who contributes most freely and heartily for the home church? Is it not the family that stands by the church paper, and that has been taught the joy of regular and systematic giving?

And so, it is the wise man, be he pastor, church official, or merely a well-wisher of his kind, who is strong in his advocacy of his church paper, who assists it to enter the homes of the people in his circle of friendship, and who exerts all proper influence for the wider circulation and improvement of his own religious paper.

PRINCIPLES AND PROGRESS
OF RELIGIOUS LIBERTY
BY REV. W.W. STALEY, D.D.[1]

This note of liberty was sounded in the Jewish commonwealth, on the year of jubilee, fifteen hundred years before Christ: "Proclaim *liberty* throughout *all* the land unto *all* the inhabitants thereof." Lev. 25:10. Eight hundred years thereafter Isaiah repeated this principle: "The Lord hath sent me to proclaim *liberty* to the captive, and opening of the *prison* to them that are bound." Isa. 61:1. Jesus indorsed this message seven hundred years later when

He quoted it and said: "This day is this Scripture fulfilled in your ears." Luke 4:21, and added, "Ye shall know the truth, and the truth shall make you free; and if the Son shall make you free ye shall be free indeed." John 8: 32, 36.

A Roman jurist said, "By natural right *all* men are born *free.*" The Declaration of Independence says: "We hold these truths to be self-evident, that *all* men are created *equal;* that they are endowed by their Creator with certain unalienable rights; that among these are life, *liberty,* and the pursuit of happiness. And Article XIII of the Constitution declares that "Neither slavery nor involuntary servitude, except as a punishment for crime, whereof the party shall have been duly convicted, shall exist within the United States, or any place subject to their jurisdiction." Religious Liberty, therefore, rests on natural right, Scriptural authority, and the law of states. 1. The right to be free is inherent, for God hath made man upright; but they have sought out many inventions. Ecc. 7:29: God put man in charge of Eden and said: "Dress it and keep it." He

[1] Delivered on Wednesday evening, September 16th, in the North Congregational church. Dr. Staley is pastor of the Christian church at Suffolk, Va.

gave him "dominion" over all the earth. And when Jesus founded His kingdom, He entrusted it to man and thus recognized his right and capacity to be free. This inherent right has burned upon the altar of human consciousness from the beginning, and its fires will never go out till all nations and all races are at liberty. Like pure water under the weight of the mountain it will work its way out to bless humanity. It is the germ of emancipation, for man is not yet free. 2. This principle is universal in its application. *All* men are sovereigns; and all men may be kings and priests unto God. Only nations where the *lowest* may become the *highest* are free. Liberty was unknown till Christianity began the struggle of many centuries with those worst of human evils—slavery and serfdom; and some of the fairest nations have been kept out of the march of human progress by Mohammedan and other false religions. The right to be free is the birthright of all nations; but amendments to Constitutions cannot set men at liberty; civil freedom may leave men in moral chains a thousand times worse than civil bondage. 3. This principle introduces a moral force that brings order out of disorder; unity out of complexity. The rule of *one man,* or *one idea* is tyranny; but when millions of men think, speak, and act, without human restraint, the world enjoys liberty. Complexity generates unity, when it obeys law. The industrial activities of this age are more complex, yet more unified, than in any age. It is the working together of a thousand intelligent forces that unifies all. What makes the vast universe of harmony is obedience to gravity; and that which will make the race one and free is love.

Europe had been subject to the Roman Church from the fourth century, and in the tenth century she assumed to "lord it over men's consciences." But when several states of Europe renounced the power of the Pope, at the Reformation, Protestant kings and governments assumed authority in religion. Civil states claimed the right to rule the church, its creed, ministry, offices, ordinances, and hence the *"state church."* Up to this time either the church controlled the state, or the state, the church. The struggle for separation was a struggle for religious liberty. Modern Europe emerges from the dark ages in a fight for separation. Christian civilization rests on this principle which is working out human freedom. It is a slow process, but it must finally win a great victory.

Guizot declares that the Crusades were the first European event; that never before had Europe been moved by the same sentiment; that not till then did Europe exist. This was a large factor in the emancipation of Europe. Rome had little communication with the people and remote states previous to the Crusades. The Crusaders stopped in Rome, saw her manners, policies, personal interest in religious disputes, and discovered her spirit. Besides this, they probably brought to Europe from the East the compass, gunpowder, printing, and new ideas that broke up old conditions, emancipated the human intellect, created new states, made a wider outlook, and planted the seeds of liberty. The lamp of science and literature kept burning during the dark ages in the monk's cell; but this movement had changed the thought and desires of a continent. What the people had felt became a conscious passion, the determination to enjoy and improve what God had provided for man in creation and the gospel. The lamp in the cell gave place to the sun in the heavens. Knowledge passed from the *few* to the *many,* and that meant progress in liberty. When Christianity entered Rome, it was a nation of slaves. A proposition in the Senate to designate slaves by dress was rejected lest the slaves might outnumber the freemen. The torture of slaves was the sport of masters and guests; and not till Christianity tempered justice did slaves have recourse to Roman courts of law. The light of Christianity opened the eyes of mankind and, step by step, slavery yielded to freedom. Another fruit of religious influence on Roman law was that in the marriage of a free man to a serf woman the children followed the free parent; and the same was true under Anglo-Saxon law. The great emancipator of the world is Jesus Christ. Throughout European and English history, serfdom and slavery gradually yield to liberty and love. This same spirit, put an end to "private war" in Germany and prepared the way for peace. Some one has said: "that all human power bears within itself a natural vice, a principle of feebleness and abuse which renders it necessary that it should be limited." But all divine power bears within itself the spirit of nobility and liberty.

Religion is the dominant force in all nations and ages. In Egypt it built its monuments along the Nile; in Greece it created the fine arts; in Rome it erected its temple of power; in Palestine it wrote its book. The religion of a nation determines its capacity to be free; religious liberty is, therefore, primary and fundamental, for no other religion has given liberty to mankind. The Mohammedan can never be free because his religion yokes him to tyranny, polygamy, and war. Modern nations can be estimated by their worship; and freedom in worship includes all freedom.

The Reformation was a great step in religious liberty, and the building of St. Peters furthered this movement. The sale of indulgences prepared the people to receive the new teaching. When Tetzel was selling indulgences in Wittenberg, a man bought the privilege to chastise a man against whom he had a grudge—that man was Tetzel himself whose appeal to the magistrate was refused.

When Luther aroused Europe by his doctrines of justification by faith; the use and authority of the Scriptures: and the right of private judgment in their interpretation; the chains began to fall from those that were bound. This movement took different forms under different leaders in different countries, but it was one bold stroke for liberty, and four centuries of progress justify the fierce battle more decisive than Marathon, Waterloo, or Gettysburg. Since that victory, the world has seen only fragments of human creeds and ecclesiastical tyranny. The world is not free yet; but it is freer than when Jesus died on Calvary, and freer than when Luther dared all for Christ. "The root of all religion is the passion to be free," and to become like Jesus Christ is to enjoy liberty. The Reformation brought men nearer to God and set in motion intellectual and moral forces that convulsed Europe; then crossed the Atlantic and kindled an unquenchable fire in the western world. But in the wake of this daring for liberty came persecution, torture, and death. "Men have always enjoyed liberty of conscience; but the liberty of speech and act brought the thumbscrew, the rack and winding-sheet of flame." But the Reformation emancipated the human mind and laid the foundation of religious liberty on the Rock of Ages; and now millions of Protestants worship God without human restraint. In Italy and Spain, where the Reformation did not take root, little progress has been made in liberty, liberal ideas or liberal laws.

The Inquisition played an important part in the religious history of the sixteenth century and by excesses reacted in favor of the Reformation and religious liberty. From the day when Luther publicly burnt at Wittenberg the bull of Leo X., containing his condemnation, 1520, and formally separated himself from the Romish Church, to the treaty of Westphalia, 1648, there were two classes of states in Europe, Catholic and Protestant, and these were arrayed against each other in bitter hostility. But from this treaty Catholics and Protestants reciprocally acknowledged each other, and states were not classified by religion, but by their external policy and relations. The cruelties inflicted by the inquisition strengthened rather than weakened the new faith, and every new invention of torture quickened and intensified the struggle for liberty.

But in spite of the eternal hunger of the human soul for liberty, the *church* in some form, barred the way of progress for centuries, even in England. None but professors of the established church were eligible *to public* employment, even after the Reformation. Severe penalties against Catholics and non-conformists alike were continued. Under Charles II, 1349-87, only those receiving the communion of the established church were eligible to office. Religious tests for admission to English universities remained down to 1871; and there is no treatment of religious liberty in the Britannica. It is in its infancy still in that great nation.

All longings, struggles, and progress in religious liberty converge and flower in these United States. It is a principle in this country that what is religious is necessarily beyond governmental control. Religious liberty here is absolute, an inherent right of the soul. All denominations are equal and free in the eye of the law. Within the limits of public peace full liberty of thought, speech, and act is granted by the Constitution. "No religious test shall ever be required as a qualification to any office or public trust under the United States. Congress shall make no law respecting the establishment of religion or prohibiting the free exercise thereof." Absolute religious liberty is the contribution of the United States to the world. Even the Roman Catholic colony of Maryland passed the "toleration act" in 1649, giving liberty of conscience to all accepting the cardinal doctrines of Christianity. Religious tolerance was incorporated in the charter of 1832, before Rhode Island which was long credited with being the first state in the world to incorporate in its organic law and to practice religious liberty. Roger Williams contended, however, that the state leave all men—Catholic, Jew, Protestant —absolutely free; and the state of Rhode Island became the cradle of religious liberty. A noted English divine said:

> Toleration will make the kingdom a chaos, is a grand work of the devil, is a most transcendental, Catholic, and fundamental evil;

and the sainted Rutherford wrote:

> We regard the toleration of all religions as not far removed from blasphemy,

But Milton, Cromwell and Sir Henry Lane stood boldly for toleration. When Roger Williams stepped from the brave ship, "Lyon," he brought soul-liberty to this hemisphere and to this infant nation. John. Fiske says:

> That Williams was the first to conceive thoroughly, and carry out consistently, in the face of strong opposition, a theory of religious liberty broad enough to win the assent and approval of advanced thinkers of the present day.

Wm. Penn was another of these great men who founded a state on this principle and inspired mankind with the reality of brotherhood. Under the universal idea of religious liberty, people of every land and creed in Europe flocked to Pennsylvania and crowded the banks of the Delaware with a prosperous and happy community; and that spirit has leavened this nation. The statue of Penn crowns the great City Hall in Philadelphia, and rises higher than any other statue above the earth, and fittingly signifies that no other statesman has reached him or equaled him. There his statue stands as a mute witness to the progress of religious liberty.

Besides these men of God, who planted the good seed of religious liberty in fertile virgin soil, two great institutions perpetuate and spread the doctrines and benefits of this heaven-born truth.

The public free school is one great teacher and advocate of liberty and, in-so-far as teachers are Christian, religious liberty is engraved upon the heart and burned into the conscience of American youth; and this means that some time it will reach all nations, for the "stars and stripes" will follow the "banner of the cross" to the end of the world. This army of teachers, plus the army of Sunday-school teachers, is mightier than the standing armies of Europe for it is the army of light and liberty. As the revival of learning broke the spell of the "dark ages," so the principle of religious liberty, radiating from the school houses of America, will enlighten the world and help to set it free.

Again, the religious press, whose beginning this occasion celebrates, in its hundredth year, is the advocate and distributor of this fundamental idea. The great things of this age are so vast that they encircle the globe. The wires of communication girdle the world. We speed across continents like birds in their flight. We fly across the ocean in luxury that outrivals the palaces of oriental princes. We read today what transpired in London yesterday. Our table is supplied by two hemispheres. Paris and St. Petersburg are nearer to us than Washington was to Jefferson when he wrote the "Declaration of Independence." What modern discovery and invention have done for the world; the religious press has done for religious liberty. The real liberty of the English press dates from the Fox

Libel Act in 1792, the very year that James O'Kelly initiated the movement that ultimate in the Christian Church. The religious press is the mightiest force in the progress of religious liberty. It has opened the eyes of mankind; unstopped the deaf ears of the ages; flooded the realms of darkness with light; unfettered conscience and emancipated the mind; imparted moral principle to the secular press, politics, and American citizenship. Its work in the field of temperance, social reform, and denominational fraternity has been commensurate with the age. Church Federation would be unknown without its help. Its silent and wholesome messages touch humanity like sunshine and rain. Its line is gone out through all the earth, its words to the end of the world. And the "religious newspaper" which has wrought such wonders, is the contribution of the Christian Church to the *"world;"* and it was the seed of a tree under whose wide-spreading branches millions have found help.

Signs of progress are now seen in the east. The Sultan of Turkey has now and then admitted Christian men to his councils, as Swartz in India, and Verbeck in Japan, and has found them wise and impartial; and, if he really means to grant a constitutional government to his millions of subjects, it means great advance in civil and religious liberty; for the young Turks are liberal in the extreme.

Russia, with a population of a hundred and fifty million souls, has been under the dominion of the Greek Catholic Church and it is stated upon good authority that probably less than seven million constitute enlightened Russia. There are less than six million students in all the schools of the empire. The rate of illiteracy is 73 to 100. But on Easter Day, 1908, Czar Nicholas issued an edict of reform in these words:

> We ordain that the falling away from the orthodox faith to any Christian confession of faith shall not give ground for any persecution, and shall not work disastrous consequences to the personal or civic rights of such a person . . . We order that wherever instruction is given in the religion of the non-orthodox Christian confessions, the same shall be given in the mother-tongue of the scholars." "Any sect numbering fifty persons, whose aims are not immoral, or having tenets like refusal to do military service, can apply for and shall receive permission to organize churches, conduct services, build schools and elect clergy, who shall be exempt from military service, and be entitled to wear vestments and perform baptism, marriage, and other sacraments."

Out of these have come new movements to spread evangelical truth in a Christian non-confessional spirit. Thus, it is seen that religious liberty is creeping into all the nations and is destined to cover the earth as the waters cover the sea.

But we are not to the end of religious liberty. We dare not claim that religious bodies, large and small, stand on equality yet in this country. Many barriers lie across the path of perfect religious liberty; but Christendom *feels* that it is *right,* and *right must prevail.* Bigotry and pride, selfishness and sin, must some day yield to this angel of freedom and this magnet of love; and this nation must first *realize* this great boon and then *teach* it to the *world.* All liberty is rooted in religious liberty; and no man can *be* his best nor *do* his best till he is *free.* Great progress has been made, but as the Lord said to Joshua of the promised land, "There remaineth yet very much land to be possessed."

Our forefathers wrought in the face of famine and cold, wild Indians and the fierce bigots of the church, and laid the foundation deep in the truth and we should work for its consummation among men. They planted the cross first on bleak Cape Henry's shore and then—

> *On Jamestown Isle they did new altars raise,*
> *Crude at the first, but with high purpose bent,*
> *And there again with heartsome hymns of praise,*
> *They worshipped Thee. O God, with one consent.*
> *So thus 'tis seen, it needs not to be proved,*
> *That in this glorious land, where they were free,*
> *Their first thought was of Him, Whom well they loved,*
> *Their glory was "Religious liberty"*

UNIVERSALIST CHURCH
Where Thursday Forenoon Session was held.

ZION'S HERALD
BY REV. A.J. NORTHRUP, PH.D.[1]

It is my privilege this morning to speak for *Zion's Herald,* a unique figure in Methodist journalism, and, because of its long career as a fashioner of opinion and as an instrument of reform, worthy of a place among the notable periodicals of the church, celebrated here.

In its organic relation our *Herald* stands apart from the other great journals of Methodism. They belong to the system; *Zion's Herald* is unofficial, and the editor therefore is independent. Rugged independence is stamped upon its whole history. When-

ever restricted coercion has been attempted, the editor has been able to reply with a sturdy disregard shown by Amos, that journalist of old, who when commanded, "Flee thee away into the land of Judah, and there eat bread and prophesy there," replied, "I am neither an official journalist nor of the school of official journalists. The Lord took me as I followed the flock, and the Lord said unto me, Go, prophesy unto My people Israel."

While officially unrestricted, and combining the sturdiness of ancient prophet with the rugged independence of modern puritan, the *Herald* through almost a century has been consistently loyal to Wesleyan teachings. So that, while our denomination of more than three million communicants may properly boast of a number of great newspapers, *Zion's Herald,* dominated by conviction only and influenced by New England ideals, stands not among New

[1] Delivered on Thursday morning, September 17th, in the Universalist church. Mr. Northrup represented Methodist journalism in New England, speaking directly for *Zion's Herald,* of Boston, Mass.

Englanders alone, but among a much wider constituency as the highest interpreter of Methodist doctrines and life.

Although independent, *Zion's Herald* is not without an organic foundation both sane and stable and well within our denomination. In order to represent the paper, we must emphasize the Boston Wesleyan Association, by whom the editor is chosen and under whose direction the journal is published. We have here a body instituted in 1831, and incorporated since 1854, of twenty New England Methodist laymen, men of business standing and true New England culture, and also believing tremendously in the mission of Methodism to New England.

While each of our six patronizing conferences sends, yearly, representatives, both lay and ministerial, to the annual meetings of the Association, who through suggestive criticisms aid much, still the burden of management ultimately rests upon this body alone. The splendid success of the *Herald,* therefore, must be attributed largely to the discernment and moral steadfastness of the members of this Association, and to the unreserved devotion with which they have given their services from the beginning, absolutely without compensation.

The achievements of the Association incidental to the publication of the *Herald* are noteworthy. In 1869 the Association purchased property on Bromfield Street, and in 1870 erected in the very heart of Boston, a five-story building occupying ten thousand feet of land, assessed today at $600,000, affording not only a permanent and suitable home for the *Herald* publishing plant, not merely offices and rooms for denominational interests, including a spacious hall, free for the Monday Boston Preachers' meeting, but, what has been of vital importance denominationally, providing a rallying place in Boston for the Methodism of New England, so that, through the publishers of this paper, Methodism, although the youngest of the larger denominations in Boston, was the first to provide there a building for general denominational purposes.

Of yet keener interest is the fact that all the financial profits are devoted by the Association to the support of the worn-out preachers of the six conferences in New England, their wives, widows and orphans. While to those who are familiar with the financial difficulties involved in the publication of a religious newspaper, it is not to the discredit of the great official *Advocates* of our denomination that their establishment has cost our church some two hundred thousand dollars, still we do record a remarkable achievement when we state that the publication of *Zion's Herald* has never cost Methodism a dollar, and that within the time of the present editorial administration alone, the publishers have paid over to the Methodist veterans of the cross in New England, at least fifty thousand dollars.

But the matters of financial profits and their distribution are incidents merely of the administration. The one great purpose of the Association is the publication of the *Herald*. What should be the mission of such a paper? There is an exceedingly cramped notion of a religious newspaper which supposes its mission to be the delivery of a dogmatic religious exhortation. Such journals we have had, packed with biblical quotations, red-hot with fanatical zeal, marked by amazing omissions and distortions of facts, appealing mightily to a few of narrowed soul, but, withal, prolific sources of skepticism. Such "journalism" is a libel, not only upon religion, but upon the newspaper business.

The religious journal must be a *newspaper,* alert and comprehensive. Wherever intellectual interests are aroused, and wherever history is being made, the editor must be immediately on the field. One omission, or one belated notice of an important event may be tolerated; but a repetition of the offense puts the paper out of the race.

But the editor of the religious newspaper is something incomparably more than a newsmonger. He is a man of prophetic utterance. Herein is to be found the charter of religious journalism. The present public need here is something appalling. The average reader, buried in the enormous daily with its jungle of confused and confusing events, is hopelessly bewildered and even stultified. The cry has gone forth for a Daniel in the newspaper world, who can "make interpretations and dissolve doubts."

The daily press, great as it is, consists in the main of newsmongers, content to thrust events upon us; there are among them only a few men under whose hands events become illustrative and purposive. As a high example of the secular journalist towering incomparably above *the* newsmonger, is the career of the late Mr. Godkin of the *Nation,* who for more than thirty years shaped the political opinions of leading statesmen in America. The religious journalist is not merely to repeat the catechism, but is to grow in his readers a living catechism, to train them into the habit of reading in events, God and the cardinal truths of religion.

Not only must past and present be correctly interpreted, but by means of stern logic coupled with prophetic intuition this man must see and portray, in bold and accurate outlines, the events that are to be.

With such a conception of the prophetic mission of the paper, its importance and power become greatly magnified, so that we are in accord with the Methodist bishop, who said: "If the apostle Paul were on earth today, he would be the editor of a newspaper."

To claim that *Zion's Herald* has perfectly and uniformly attained to this ideal would assume too much, but we are within the bounds of the simple truth when we say that the editor and management have always been aware of its prophetic mission. At times the paper has conspicuously demonstrated this fact, and through its long career it certainly has approached the goal as closely as any other journal in the field.

Zion's Herald is the oldest Methodist newspaper in the world. To this fact we attach only incidental value. Senility nodding at the fireside and driveling over an empty past merits no honor. Our main contention, therefore, is for the virility of this paper rather than any antecedence in date of origin. Still, there is this to be said, that *Zion's Herald* was in the field to fight some of the hottest battles for religious liberty long before many of the younger journals of our denomination were born.

The first Methodist paper published was the *Weekly History,* a paper started in 1740 in connection with the White- field Calvinistic movement. As early as 1815 the *New England Missionary Magazine* was begun at Concord, N.H., but not until 1823 was there published anywhere in the world a Methodist newspaper destined to survive until the present. This paper was the *Zion's Herald,* the first issue of which appeared January 9, 1823. While the

Herald's claim to priority of origin over all other Methodist newspapers has been disputed on the ground that for four years (1827-1831) the paper was published in New York in connection with the *Christian Advocate and Journal* as the *Christian Advocate and Journal and Zion's Herald,* the disputant is reasonably silenced by the simple fact that the *Herald* office is in possession of a continuous file of the paper, one week excepted, from January 9, 1823, until now. This file I have seen and examined.

In the first issue of the *Herald* I observed, at the head of a brief sermon this text, "The Lord thy God reigneth." This text providentially is set at the head of the paper as the text for its preachment of nearly a century.

Contrasting the conditions existing in 1823 with those of the present, we are startled at the revelation of achievements wrought. At that time, there was neither civil nor religious liberty for white or black. For ten years after the establishment of the *Herald,* Massachusetts had her state church. Dissenters were barely tolerated, often insulted and even attacked. The doctrine of "Free Grace" was counted a heresy black and damnable. Not only was the black man in chains, not only did bishops reckon him among their chattels, but by a theological dogma, exceedingly popular, anathemas were prepared for any who should hint that the negro ought to be emancipated.

At this time the national spirit had not yet been developed, and everywhere bitter sectional jealousies prevailed. The great questions of temperance and of the equal rights of woman lay slumbering in a public conscience not yet awakened. And in this jubilee season, in the very proper exultation over the wonderful theological, social and political transformation here in New England, we are to remember that in every great battle waged since its inception, *Zion's Herald* has always been conspicuous in the fight, and always on the side of humanity, liberty and righteousness. A glance at particular instances in the reform movement of the past century will vindicate the claim.

Zion's Herald as an exponent of the Methodist doctrines of "Free Grace" has aided in the transformation of New England theology. The theology of the orthodox churches has become

Methodistic. John Wesley and not John Calvin prevails. You will remember how less than a century *ago,* the orthodox Christianity here in New England, held that the saved were saved because God willed it, that the lost remained impenitent, and would be lost because God willed it. To assent to such horrible doctrines, stultifying the human conscience, and impeaching divine goodness meant theological respectability. But to maintain as the Methodists did, that God desired all men to be saved, was to be a pronounced religious and social pariah.

Methodism is not to be held responsible for all the theologies to be discovered in New England. For ultra-Unitarian views, the horrible theological dogmas of that day are responsible. As the frenzied occupants often rush half- naked from the burning dwelling, only to be frozen in the winter's cold, so, many have rushed from rigid Calvinism into a denial of the essentials of Christianity. But there is in New England today a normal theology, not a theology of reaction, wherein the child of God is clothed and sheltered, a theology in which more and more there is a practical unanimity among the denominations. One cannot read the consistent reiterations of the *Herald* and note the increase of Methodist communicants, together with this transformation in theology, without conceding the *Herald* some part in the victory. Then too, *Zion's Herald* has been the exponent of a doctrine once derided, but now coming into almost universal acceptance, that of a "knowable religion," the religion of experience.

In the advocacy of social and political reform *Zion's Herald* has been a notable figure. In the anti-slavery agitation, the *Herald* assumed a position often then of unenviable unpopularity, which now constitutes a most enviable record. The history of the abolition movement in this country cannot be properly recorded without including at least one notable issue of the paper. The issue of October 28, 1835, belongs properly as an integral part of a most important chapter in the history of the nation. From 1830 to 1850, Boston, although originally the hot-bed of freedom, was ruled by slavery. Thursday, October 21, 1835, a mob composed of "gentlemen of standing" incited by the secular press, made the notorious, dastardly attempt upon the person and life of Mr. Garrison. The entire secular press of Boston were with the mob in these atrocious proceedings against the leaders of the abolition movement. The religious press also, with two notable exceptions, gave their sympathy to the mob. The *Christian Standard,* now extinct, and *Zion's Herald* alone of the papers in Boston spoke fearlessly in denunciation of the outrage. The scathing censure visited by the editor of the *Herald* that day upon the secular press, upon the mob and their sympathizers does one's heart good. I am sure that neither Amos nor Ezekiel could have spoken better. Through a greater part of the antislavery agitation which later waxed hot in the church, *Zion's Herald,* withstanding the advice of certain bishops and the pressure of general conference, opened its columns freely to a discussion of the issue. Dr. Abel Stevens says: "It was the only church paper really open to abolitionists during the long anti-slavery struggle."

The advanced position taken by the *Herald* in the reforms of church polity within the Methodist Episcopal Church, such as equal lay representation and the admission of women into the general conference, were of inestimable value to the movements indicated, and give weight to our assertion as to the high leadership maintained by this paper within the denomination.

From the time of its first issue when abstinence from alcoholic beverages was derided, and the prohibition of their sale scarcely thought of, until in this day prohibition seems surely coming as an earnest of the millennial dawn, *Zion's Herald* has steadily, widely and with unwavering earnestness advocated total abstinence and prohibition.

Zion's Herald has shown itself keenly alive also to the social movements of our day, and has encouraged the church

to exert a more sensitive sympathy and to seek to acquire a more intelligent grasp of the actual needs of working men.

The *Herald* is not unworthy of the eulogy spoken by Ex-Governor Claflin, of Massachusetts, who said:

> I want a paper true to the genius of New England Methodism, independent, yet loyal, literary and yet spiritual, fully abreast and in touch with the social problems of the day. I have never seen greater devotion to duty than in the entire editorial corps of this paper.

The list of editors includes sixteen names, among whom are to be found men of the brightest genius. To repeat the entire list is without profit; to properly review the individual career of each is impossible; still even this outline sketch of the history of this journal would be incomplete without a glance at some of the great personalities in the editorial chair, who have made the paper. Among the greatest is Dr. Abel Stevens, the genius in pen portraiture, whose pen served both as camera and kinetoscope, who added to the peculiar vividness of his editorials a delicious, scholarly and literary flavor; a born historian, the greatest in our church.

Daniel Wise—an instance where names are really prophetic, a man great in goodness, also an easy and felicitous writer, a leader among the old-school journalists.

E.O. Haven, versatile, equally strong as a preacher, teacher, editor or president of a great university, yet because of a certain coldness of disposition, wanting in his hold upon the popular heart.

Gilbert Haven stands as the favorite Methodist radical of New England. Although engrossed in a dozen reform movements, he is most widely known as the intense friend of the negro. While at times lacking in balance and comprehensiveness, as an agitator he was without a peer. His biographer says of him:

> He went into the editorial chair consecrated and ordained to utter all the great convictions of his soul as to the vices and sins, the duties and needs of the church and nation.

He was a radical on the question of slavery, caste, temperance, co-education, women's rights, equal representation of the laity in the Methodist Episcopal Church, and in his zeal for the evangelical faith against the proud and dangerous liberalism of his day. He advocated Wesleyan doctrines and the institutions peculiar to Methodism under high pressure.

Loyalty to the truth does not permit me to omit the name of the present editor, Dr. Charles Parkhurst. Twenty years ago, it became evident that the *Herald* was losing its grip upon the mind and convictions of its constituency. The publishers, therefore, resolved upon extreme measures. They found in New Hampshire; a young man almost unknown, ignorant of the technicalities of editorship. They told him not only to revive the *Herald,* but to bring it forward to meet the strenuous and exacting demands of a new journalistic age. This he has done. Under him, because of his heroic devotion, and that of his assistants, his superb power of editorial management, his comprehensiveness and alertness, often amounting to anticipation, the *Herald* has become informational, virile, and creative of conviction, and we are not surprised to learn that within the past year the circulation has increased to the highest point within its history.

Never have* the difficulties in the way been more subtle and dangerous than within the past quarter of a century. The editor has been obliged to steer his ship between two rocks. On the one side is the Scylla of a dogmatic literalism, or hyper-orthodoxy insisting upon literal biblical interpretation, clamoring against all thorough biblical investigation and blocking the way of scientific progress. On the other side is the Charybdis of scientific dogmatism, and Christ-less liberalism. The wisdom and tact required for leadership under such conditions need no elaboration here. With an independence that has exasperated both enemies and friends he has steered wisely and well.

Zion's Herald, always fundamentally orthodox and evangelical, while not weakening in its mission of agitation, and losing nothing in the literary sense, with the ripening years of the editor becomes more and more rich in its spiritual emphasis and power.

UNITARIAN JOURNALISM
BY REV. ALFRED GOODING[1]

I am not attempting to take the place of Mr. Batchelor who would have given you a very interesting and instructive half-hour. I want simply to say a few words concerning Unitarian Journalism in order that that important branch of religious journalism in America may not go wholly unnoticed at this conference.

It was entirely natural for the founders of American Unitarianism to find in journalism one of the most effective means to the strengthening and propagating of their religious faith and opinions. They were largely men of marked literary ability, skillful reasoners and accomplished writers, and they* naturally sought to spread their theological views through the medium of public print as well

as of public speaking. As early as 1813, Channing. Lowell and Parkman planned a monthly magazine that should be liberal in its character but not sectarian or dogmatic. The first number of the *Christian Disciple,* as it was called, appeared, under the editorship of Rev. Noah Worcester, in May, 1813. It was not a controversial publication but rather humanitarian, devoting much space to the temperance reform and to the condemnation of slavery and of war. In 1824 it passed into the hands of Rev. John G. Palfrey, the well-known historian, who changed its title to that of *The Christian Examiner.* "Gradually it became the organ of the higher intellectual life of the Unitarians and gave expression to their interest in literature, general culture and the phi-

<hr>

[1] Delivered in the Universalist church on Wednesday morning. September 17th. Mr. Gooding is pastor of the Unitarian church in Portsmouth, N.H. Rev. George Batchelor, the editor of *The Christian Register,* was detained by illness, and Mr. Gooding was called upon to occupy the time in behalf of "Unitarian Journalism."

lanthropies, as well as theological knowledge." (Cooke's "Unitarianism in America"). The best scholars conducted it; the best writers contributed to it.

For nearly fifty years it performed its important work under the editorship of such men as James Walker, William Ware, Ezra S. Gannett, George Putnam and Edward Everett Hale. "Its final decease in 1869 was a serious loss, not to the denomination alone, but to the cause of enlightened mind."

Contemporary with the *Examiner,* but as a more popular vehicle of religious thought, the Unitarian body has maintained and still maintains the *Christian Register.* The first number of the *Register* appeared on April 20, 1821, and the paper has been issued every week since August 24th, of that year. Among its early contributors were: Kirkland, Story, Edward Everett, Furness, Palfrey, Gannett, Bancroft, Sparks, Pierpont and Lowell.

Cooke, in his "Unitarianism in America," says of the *Register:* "It has always been a well-conducted periodical, representing a wide range of interests, and admirably suited to interpret the temper and spirit of a rational religion." It is our only periodical that has maintained an unbroken existence from the early days of Unitarianism in

America. Many others have appeared; there is a long list of them; but the terms of their publication have been more or less brief. They have often represented local interests and needs. The *Register,* I suppose, may be called the organ of the American Unitarian Church. It publishes what is important for its readers to know—the affairs of the denomination, its doings and interests. It is ably edited, carefully printed, free from every sort of objectionable advertisement, and its contributors are men of ideas and of literary skill. As a religious journal, it suits me. I have read it faithfully for nearly thirty years. If other denominational organs are as good as the *Register,* I am sure that they must be to you, as that is to me, a source of immense encouragement, instruction and inspiration.

THE CENTENNIAL OF RELIGIOUS JOURNALISM
BY REV. ANSON TITUS[1]

It is ours to give the greeting of the publishing interests, Historical Society and those who cherish the generous faith of the Universalist Church. Our Church issued from the social life, theological controversy and teeming times following the war of the American Revolution. Our early believers, for the most part, came out of the Baptist Church. They were the friends, neighbors and of the same household of those who became Free Baptists and Christians.

The words "liberty" and "freedom" were grafted from the vocabulary of the political world. The questions uppermost were concerning the "liberty of the spirit," "the authority of the Bible" and the character of God and man. The fragments of Protestantism at the beginning of the nineteenth century presented a curious picture. The question of the destiny of the human race was not the most important one in the discussion. It was one, but not the entire issue or bone of contention. The times which made possible the founding and rapid growth of the Methodist Church, and the breaking up of the more ancient Baptist organizations, made possible the beginnings of the Universalist order of believers.

The earliest fairly regular publication of Universalist believers was *The Berean,* or *Scripture Searcher,* in Boston, 1802-1809. It was irregular in publication. It was succeeded in 1811 and 1812 by *The Gospel Visitant,* published by a group of ministers of whom Thomas Jones of Gloucester, Mass., Hosea Ballou, then of Portsmouth, N.H., and Edward Turner of Salem, Mass., were chief

---

[1] Delivered on Thursday morning in the Universalist church. Mr. Titus is connected with the Universalist Historical Society and himself an editor.

contributors and publishers. But this also was irregular and continued only two years.

It was not, however, until July 1, 1819, soon after the removal of Hosea Ballou to Boston, that *The Universalist Magazine* began its weekly publication, and has weekly continued, under different names, in Boston until the present time. *The Universalist Magazine* antedates several other publications which have been prominently mentioned. The constituency of the Universalist body was not behind in founding its religious journal. It has ever been its pride that it was a pioneer in intelligent discussion of the large questions concerning God, duty and mankind. A month later, Aug. 1, 1819, *The Christian Messenger* was issued in Philadelphia; in 1820 *The Gospel Herald* was established in New York City; in 1821 *The Christian Repository* was established in Woodstock, Vt.; in 1821 *The Christian Intelligencer* was founded in Portland, Me.; in 1821, *The Religious Inquirer* in Hartford, Conn.; in 1823 *The Gospel Advocate* in Buffalo, N.Y., and in 1827 *The Star in the West* at Eaton, Ohio.

There are several other and later journals of local character; but combination became the habit, so that finally it resolved to *The Trumpet and Freeman* of Boston, *The Christian Ambassador* of New York State, *The Christian Repository* of Vermont, *The Gospel Banner* of Maine, *The Star of the West* of Cincinnati, and *The New Covenant* of Chicago. These journals wrought a noble service, and in the course of years, a further combination came looking to the larger welfare of the church, in *The Universalist Leader* of today. The earlier journals were private interests, and the combination of these private interests created the Universalist Publishing House of Boston. The Publishing House conserves the welfare and prosperity of the church at large. Their interests are mutual, though entirely separate from the corporate existence of State or General Convention.

The journals of the Universalist Church have, without exception, taken advanced grounds on the questions of anti-slavery, temperance, reforms in social living, upbuilding of educational institutions and the nourishing of sources of moral culture. Our journals, in common *with* many another, have been aggressive in putting *forth our* doctrines and policies. The controversial *spirit did not* enter the columns of our journals until a number *of* years after their founding. Our opposers were willing to let us alone, and we attended to our own affairs; but from the time of the great revival in 1827-1832 the spirit of controversy was forced upon us by the fierce and too frequently unjust accusations of revivalists. From this time forth until the Civil War, the controversial spirit was a leading factor, and this not only from our own love of controversy, but the love of controversy on the part of our opposers. The columns of every religious journal had the controversial habit, even to the neglect of the weightier matters of the law.

The word "orthodox," strictly a New England word, was taken to themselves by those who called other people "heterodox." The word "evangelical" was assumed during the great revival by those who held every one else to be "unevangelical." But these are growing to be with the years, relative terms. They do not mean much today. The word "liberal" has grown flat and stale, and confident are we that these several words in time will become obsolete, and cast as rubbish to the void. The better day is coming. The larger affairs of the kingdom of God demand a larger charity and closer fellowship in all things essential. The churches of today are praying larger prayers, are preaching larger thoughts and making demands upon believers never before uttered. The journals of the church of a living God were never so alive as today. We are fairly familiar with the words, as they come warm from the editorial sanctums of the religious journals of the nation, and confident are we that the kingdom of God is coming at a more rapid rate than ever.

The editor is the blessed ally of the minister; the journal is the educator, inspirer and comforter of the home; the journal is the right hand of every advancing cause of God. It is fitting therefore that the religious journals of the church recognize this century of their existence, their growth and their power. Their influence has only just begun; the splendid inheritance has only been feebly appreciated; but a new century is at hand; the field is white for a new and finer harvest. The call is for the divine right of the churches getting together in all their vast concerns. Variety there always will be, and charity always must be; but hand in hand the living God calls for all to hasten His kingdom into the hearts of mankind.

Elias Smith was a man for his time and generation. He was an easy victim for every wind of doctrine. He was constructed on that plan. The whole gamut of controversy it was his privilege to sound. To keep track of him theologically was most difficult. The Universalist Church has its share of him. He was in its fellowship at different times; his first, as he says in his memorable Autobiography, was for "fifteen days." He published in 1819 a book in advocacy of doctrines held by Hosea Ballou. He was a physician of the body as well, if not better, than of the soul. He lectured on his system of doctoring (Thompsonian) throughout New England, and never gave up the privilege of proclaiming the gospel as he understood it. With all his wavering amid the doctrines of the church, he ever clung close to the Bible as an authority from God. as possessing an inspired revelation from God; he held to liberty and an open Bible. The charge of infidelity was never intelligently made against him. Jesus continued his Lord and Master and the Bible his book of life. In 1840, while residing in Providence, R.I., in his age, but still vigorous in mind, he caught anew the vision of the Savior's conquest over every sin, and enemy of God, and found a comfort he never before realized. He passed forward to the home immortal in the summer of 1846, at the home of a daughter in Lynn, Mass., and his funeral was conducted by the eminent Boston divine, Rev. Sebastian Streeter.

Be it further said that with all his theological migrations, Mr. Smith remained a friend of Hosea Ballou whose neighbor he was in Portsmouth and Boston. The words of Rev. Lemuel Willis, in a chapter in his "Recollections,"[1] upon Elias Smith, whom he knew intimately for many years, are of worth today. He says, "Elias Smith was always an honest man." Elias Smith had a temperament different from many, but was ever honest, outspoken and earnest. He wrought a better work than he knew. He well deserves the homage of the whole church. This centennial assemblage affords an opportunity for expression; the words will pass along, and editors feeling the pulsations of this gathering will send forth the favoring message in their journals and anew will sound the homage

[1] In columns of *The Universalist.* Boston, 1876.

of the church in behalf of one of its humble laborers in the vineyard whose fruits we so well enjoy

The century of religious journalism in America is not without
interest and romance. It marks an era in the unfoldment of Christian truth, and the enforcement of Christian truths upon the lives
and characters of Christian believers. There have been many a turn
and overturn in the journals of every denomination, but from them
all have gone forth an influence for the cementing of unity, the advancement of common purposes, and the progress of principles
which betoken a great step forward in theoretical and practical
Christianity.

THE GENIUS OF THE CHRISTIAN MOVEMENT
BY REV. J. PRESSLEY BARRETT, D.D.[1]

Every thought, if made effective, must have expression; every life, if made useful, must have a purpose; and every institution, if worthy of the name, must have a plan. If any one of these factors be lacking, results are necessarily very uncertain.

It has been said that history repeats itself. If so, it is an effort to correct mistakes and regain losses.

The church idea worked somewhat in this way. Truth does not change in its essential character, but man's relation to truth is by no means so steady. The church, as well as the state, is subject to

disturbances, upheavals and even revolutions, entailing losses of the most serious nature.

No great period of history has passed without such losses to the church. This is true of both Judaism and Christianity. Judaism had its Egyptian slavery and its deliverance; the destruction of its temple and its rebuilding; Babylonish captivity and the return of the Jews to their own land; the crucifixion of the Christ and His resurrection. The Christian dispensation has witnessed persecution and martyrdom with untold losses from internal strife and opposing influences. Even the endowment of the church with world power and influence under Constantine brought great spiritual losses. It was practically the beginning of the Dark Ages.

Today, we stand face to face with the perils of a spiritually bedimmed scholarship, with a strong leaning to the practical aban-

[1] Delivered on Thursday morning, September 17th, in the Universalist church. Dr. Barrett is the editor of the *Herald of Gospel Liberty,* Dayton, Ohio.

donment of the strongholds of the Christian faith. In the midst of these disturbances the church has witnessed many a rise and fall, sometimes her thought has been wrecked; sometimes her purpose has been shaken; sometimes her plans have been upset, but in storm and sunshine she has remained the blood-bought church, and like the well-ballasted ship, she has always righted herself and continued her way for the harbor of safety.

It was in the throes of these theological upheavals that the original beauty of the church was so marred as hardly to be recognized as the institution outlined to us in the New Testament. Spiritual decline necessarily followed, continuing for many centuries. The darkness was intense and the church drifted as a ship with a broken shaft and a helpless crew. At length it pleased God to dispel this long night of ignorance and superstition. The church has been even longer in regaining, than she was in losing, her likeness to the divine ideal. The Reformation was one of a series of terrific upheavals which shook the church as a great earthquake shakes the earth. It was a necessity. As the miner breaks in pieces the ore that he may gather and treasure its rich nuggets of gold, so these theological earthquakes were just as necessary as a means of breaking up error for the liberation of pure truth.

From the conversion of Constantine to Christianity the church, perhaps unwittingly, had abandoned herself largely to the world spirit. This decline became the undoing in a large degree of the achievements of the apostolic age. On this battleground the church lost heavily and rapidly. This down grade tendency continued for more than a thousand years. At length when reaction did set in, the recovery of ancient ideals was very slow. Even in victory there was a heavy loss to the visible organization through the necessary breaking up of existing conditions.

This work of destruction had been long continued and most disastrous. Reconstruction was also slow and hazardous. With the settling of great issues came other disruptions, shaping themselves into new ideals. These were speedily followed by a multiplicity of denominations each more or less strongly set with sectarian bias,

Reformers were numerous, each leading a movement peculiar to his own conception of truth. Every reform movement became a sort of religious storm center, presenting a scene of confusion. Every such organization became a school of thought peculiar to its own genius. These gave rise to many denominations, more and more obscuring the original ideals of the true church. Hundreds of years have not been sufficient to undo the mischief thus wrought in dividing the church. Every division, instead of helping, seemed to delay the preaching of the Gospel to every creature.

Among the earliest to see the havoc thus wrought in the church of Christ, was a small group of men who lived in the closing days of the Eighteenth and in the opening days of the Nineteenth Centuries. These were James O'Kelly, Rice Haggard, Abner Jones, Elias Smith, Barton W. Stone and David Purviance. They saw, not the need of another denomination, but the necessity for the people of God to get together in the spirit of the Master after the manner of the early church. Out of this desire and purpose sprang what we call the Christian Movement.

The aim of this paper is to present briefly the thought and spirit of these men. If we are to grasp the Genius of the Christian Movement, as they launched it, we must search diligently the moral and spiritual upheavals of the days of the Reformation and the times following. If we find it, we shall discover the essential organic structure of the church and the spiritual life common in the days of the apostles. The decline of the church which followed the downfall of the Roman Empire had been slow. Its reconstruction must necessarily be slow.

These prophets of the Christian Movement sought to bring back to the common people the fresh vigor and spiritual beauty of the church as in the days when Pentecostal fires burned in every heart under the descent of the Spirit and the preaching of Peter, that again she might go forth to her legitimate work of bringing the lost world to Christ.

Necessarily many distorted ideals were thrust upon the people of God, involving many misunderstandings, mistakes and failures, but these were the losses which necessarily follow the pulling down of the old, as a preparation for rebuilding the new.

No man can do better than to live up to the light he has, or with proper effort, may get. No doubt these men made mistakes. The drift of their life service may seem too many to have been in vain, yet we must admit their labors were an important part of a great whole.

In a prayerful study of the Word of God these men caught a clear vision of the church of Christ as the Family of God, with Jesus the Elder Brother, as its head, and with the Holy Spirit as the guide to the Household of faith. In this clear vision the rights, privileges and the blessings of this spiritual kingdom were for everyone who was prepared to receive them. This household ideal was very near to the original model of the church of Christ, as outlined to us in the New Testament. This vision deepened into a conviction, the conviction ripened into a movement which, though never of great numerical or financial proportions, yet became a leader in a number of forward movements, which have exercised a large influence in the shaping of the destiny of the church of the Nineteenth Century. Such as the Introduction of the idea that the Bible is the creed, and the only creed, the church needs; the establishment of the religious newspaper; the admission of women to equal privileges in the college curriculum with men; and the name Christian as the only name the church of Christ needs.

This Movement was based upon the essential principle that the church of Christ is one in its life, in its spirit. in its character and in its work. In it every child of God has inherent and undeniable rights which no man may give and no man may take away from any trusting child of God, for if *children* then *heirs.* Their rights are by inheritance.

For this conception of the church, they were dependent upon the Bible. The principle involved has exerted a dominant influence over the organization through all its history. For more than one hundred years it has swept along the currents of religious thought as a great Gulf Stream, melting the icebergs of bigotry and sectarianism. The Bible being the creed of its faith and the rule of its practice, no Christian can be excluded from its membership. "By their fruits ye shall know them."

The truths of the Bible are fundamental. Opinions about these truths may vary so long as the variations are not specifically unchristian. This basic principle of the church necessarily gave rise to other controlling ideas which dominated the Movement everywhere.

Some of these are:

The Bible as authority on all matters of Christian life, experience and service, as the Holy Spirit may reveal them to the individual mind and heart.

We bow, not to the teachings of man, nor to a man-made theology, nor to councils, nor to Popes, but to the Word of God. We do not believe that the Bible has been decomposed, nor its authority dissolved. Nor do we believe the logic of Protestantism requires any such decomposition or dissolution.

With the Bible as man's guide in finding his way back to eternal life in Christ we associate his right to enjoy the privilege of individual interpretation of the Word for himself. Man's first approach to God is necessarily individual. No man could have been a proxy for Moses at the burning bush. He must go in person, in mind and heart. The coming of the individual to Christ involves the necessity of a personal experience. Hence the individual acceptance of Christ must depend very largely upon the Spirit's revelation of truth to the individual mind; and yet it is a fact that individual interpretation is circumscribed by well-defined limitations. No scripture must be given an un-Christian interpretation—the Spirit of Christ must permeate its every thought. Again, individual interpretation does not mean that the individual in the exercise of this right may repudiate any portion of Scripture, and this is the more important since the right of individual interpretation rests upon the full acceptance of the Bible as the Word of God. Such interpretation, therefore, must always be Christian in its spirit, scope and purpose. This gives largest liberty consistent with the teachings of the Word. It is by no means a license for uncontrolled freedom, either in thought or conduct. No one has authority to do as he pleases regardless of truth. Christian liberty is freedom to do God's will as the Spirit may make it plain to the believer as revealed in the Bible.

It has been said that true liberty has been found only in obedience to the proper restraints of life. The banks of the river keep its waters under control and in the proper channel; the planets unrestrained by the law of gravitation would wreck themselves in their own confused flights. Restraint regulates liberty and affords protection from evil— it is not a license to do evil, but a restraint from danger, binding us to the right. The man who claims liberty as his authority for doing as he pleases is already in the bondage of sin and so handicapped in his efforts to serve God or to help his fellowmen. It is said that the nightingale will not sing in a cage—she must have her God-given liberty ere her sweetest and highest note can be sounded. It is just so with the Christian—bind him in the galling chains of the teachings of men and he cannot reach the pinnacle of harmony with God. This was Paul's idea as expressed to the Corinthian church: *"Where the Spirit of the Lord is, there is liberty."*

The Christian Church does not stand for liberty apart from the truth. Her great work is to search out the truth as revealed in the word of God, and having found it, she gets her largest liberty by obedience to its requirements. The individual must obey not what the Word says to another, but what it says to him, personally. The French Revolution had as a motto: *"Liberty, Equality and Fraternity,"* and yet it became the Inspiration of sin and crime and bloodshed. It defied the laws of faith and conscience, and in anarchy precipitated a nation into the depths of skepticism. We know the wreck that followed such lawlessness. Such liberty will produce like results in the church.

The position of the Christian Church has been construed by some outsiders to mean independence of thought in defiance to the Word of God. The right and duty to follow reason, rather than revelation, has been boldly declared by the unfriendly. This is a freak of boyish scholarship, from which with love and patience, the offender may recover himself, or if not, he will go into downright infidelity.

Rev. N. Summerbell, D.D., once said:

> The Christians hold what may be called conservative orthodoxy. They strip orthodox doctrines of all popish dress and hold them in Biblical truth: but HOLD them. We do not encourage or tolerate attacks on the Bible: we stand or fall with the Bible. If the Bible be true, as we affirm, it is the foundation of all truth: If (which is impossible) the Bible

were not true, we have no business as a church, and should disband.

Loyalty is a great thought—not as applied to any human theology, but to the Word of God. As such it is the slogan of the Christian Movement—it was in the beginning of our work, it is now, and let us pray that it may be forever. Loyalty to the Word of God was not only the thought of the early leaders among us, but was largely the thought of many of the great reformers.

Martin Luther boldly repudiated human creeds, declaring that either the preacher or the layman had the right to read the Bible and judge individually of its teachings for his own life. This is essentially just what the Christians have taught from the beginning.

John Wesley also repudiated human creeds and magnified the Bible as the only authority for the church, declaring that he would "regard the authority of no writings but the inspired." It was for this liberty to be free from human dictation, and free to obey the Word of God, for which our forefathers contended.

Elias Smith, the founder of religious journalism, has said:

> Religious liberty is what my heart rejoices in, and what I long for all men to enjoy. I am bound, as a lover of mankind to instruct them and to teach them the nature of it, according to my ability and the opportunity given me. This is the glorious liberty of the children of God; begun here, to be completed at the resurrection of the just. This is the liberty which the Son of God proclaimed to captives, founded on the perfect law of liberty, wherewith Christ makes us free indeed. This liberty was first preached by Jesus Christ, next by the apostles, who learnt of Him, and was known and enjoyed by the CHRISTIANS in the days of the apostles.

The basic principle for which we stand, as a people, makes it necessary to take the Bible, and the Bible *only,* as the guide for the Christian life. This is not a *no-creed* theory, as many have claimed, —it means not that the Christians have no creed, but that they have no creed but the Bible—an all-sufficient creed. No creed at all would mean no belief, and no belief would put us outside the pale of Christianity, making us in fact no better than agnostics. Certainly, we have a creed, a precious creed—contained only in the thought of the Word. This gives us an advantage over other creeds, at least in this, we avoid confusing the commandments of God with the commandments of men, as is so often done when man attempts to formulate his individual belief into a creed for others. All Christian creeds are based on the Bible except ours—ours *is* the Bible. We object to doctrine which cannot be stated in Bible language, because the thought which cannot be stated in Bible language cannot claim the Bible as its source.

It is a fact, a lamentable fact, that the divisions of the church have arisen almost wholly from the effort of men to formulate God's thought into human creeds. Can any human creed be *better* than the Bible? Or even *equal* to the Bible? All must answer in the negative. Then why lay aside the *best* for something *not* so good? Why turn from Him in whom is light, and with whom is no darkness at all, to follow where light and darkness are so much confused?

We do not hold that Bible doctrine is *unimportant,* but just the opposite. It is vital to the life and faith and service of the believer, and equally important for the church, as a body, but we mean *Bible doctrine,* expressed in Bible language—not man's biased formulated statements of doctrine. The Christian Movement thus became a necessity with our fathers to enable them to escape endorsing and teaching the commandments of men.

One of the leading minds associated with our Movement in the Nineteenth Century, said:

> We hold truth in the words in which God gave it, prophets wrote it, Christ spoke it and the apostles taught it We will neither add to the words for popery, nor give them up for liberty. If the imperfect forms (of so-called truth) are taught in the Bible, it must be In Bible language. If that is the way God chose to teach them, that is the way we choose; if we can learn them in Bible language, we have no need of formulas. If we cannot, then we did not learn them in the Bible.

The Bible was given for man's instruction in spiritual truth by the best Teacher of the ages. If He could not teach us truth correctly, then no other need try. As we see it, the difference between the commandments of God and the formulated statements of doctrine by man is as the difference between the early morning *fog* and the clear, beautiful and pure atmosphere of a cloudless mid-day.

Not only are the formulated creed statements responsible for the divisions of the church, but we hold it largely responsible for the more modern and so-called respectable phases of unbelief. Men became so sick and tired of the creeds of men that they could not bear them any longer, and when they began to *unload,* they failed to discriminate between the Word of God and the creeds of men and both were largely discarded.

The first great victory of our pioneer leaders was gained at the foot of the Cross, when they laid aside all authority in religion except the Bible. Having regained, as they believed, the true ideal of the primitive church, the need of a name for this Movement confronted them as an immediate necessity. They readily saw that the name to serve their purpose must be ideal—scriptural. The name must be acceptable to every true believer. The denominational names already in use were considered, but failed to meet their needs, for they were not large enough to include the whole family of God. The name which should serve to identify this Movement must be big enough and broad enough to give a royal welcome to every child of God. It was indeed a perplexing problem and a vital issue.

After much prayer in conference, God gave to Rice Haggard the privilege and honor to suggest a name in every way just suited to meet their needs. In the Conference at Lebanon, Surry County, Virginia, August 4, 1794, he arose before the assembled representatives of the brotherhood and bolding aloft in his right hand a copy of the New Testament, he said:

> Brethren, this is a sufficient rule of faith and practice. By it we understand the disciples of our Lord were first called Christians, and I move that henceforth and forever the followers of Christ be known as Christians simply.

The motion prevailed unanimously, and from this time and

event, as a people, we have recognized no other name, and why should we? Did not Paul give us fair warning of the danger of party names for God's people? In I Corinthians 1:12, 13, he boldly declares:

> Now this I say that every one of you that saith, I am of Paul: and I of Apollos; and I of Cephas; and I of Christ Is Christ divided? Was Paul crucified for you, or were you baptized in His name?

That puts the philosophy of the name of the redeemed in a nutshell. He who was crucified for us—shall not *His name be ours?* Is He not our bridegroom? And can we without guilt lay aside His name for another? Let us think—let us face the facts. Before us stand Christ and Luther—whose name shall we wear? Before us stand Christ and Huss— whose name shall we wear? Before us stand Christ and Wesley —whose name shall we wear? Before us stand Christ and O'Kelly—whose name shall we wear? Shall the bride choose and wear the name of Luther, or Huss, or Wesley, or O'Kelly? Or shall she in true loyalty wear the real name of the bridegroom and after Him call herself Christian? Who are Luther and Huss and Wesley and O'Kelly? And what have they done for us? They were instruments in leading us to Christ. And what has Christ done for us? And what is He still doing for us? He died to redeem us from the curse of sin under the law, so making us heirs of God. The church is His own loved bride, all glorious within and beautiful without. Not only so, but He ever liveth to make intercession for us at the right hand of God. Ah, surely by every reasonable claim He has a right to expect us to wear His name.

Again, before us stand Christ and His ordinances—what name shall we wear? Before us stand Christ and the forms of church government—what name shall we wear? Shall *an ordinance* take first place, and *Christ* second? Shall a mere *form of church government* come first and *Christ* second? Never! He must be first—He *is* first.

It is enough. We recognize Him as our bridegroom—we wear His name as we seek to live His victorious life. Because we are spiritually married to him, we call ourselves Christians after His own beautiful name.

And we wear His name not in any invidious sense, not in any presumptuous way, but we wear it devoutly, as indicating our allegiance to Christ, and at the same time as most promotive of real brotherly love in true Christian unity and a Christ-like fellowship. It has been charged that we wear the name Christian in an exclusive sense, as though no others are Christians. The opposite is true--we wear it as the heritage of every child of God. If any refuse it, that is neither our fault, nor is it any reason why we should give it up, since a Christ-like life is a sure passport to the fellowship of our people. No other name is inclusive enough to honor our principles.

The only exclusive sense in which we wear the name Christian is in our organic relationship, and that is a logical necessity, rather than a purpose upon our part. We hold that no organization should wear the name Christian so long as the conditions of fellowship shut out from its membership any true child of God. Under that name all Christians have a right to stand, to live, and to serve.

Most certainly we readily grant that any church whose terms of fellowship are such as to cut off a part of the people of God, has a right to wear a sectarian name—for it is a sect, but it is equally true that any church whose conditions of fellowship are such as to welcome to its fellowship any and every true child of God—that church has a logical and a Scriptural right to call itself simply Christian.

The Christian Church seeks to give to the church universal a practical expression of true Christianity in its beauty and simplicity, divested of the last vestige of sectarianism to the end that the world may see Christ in us as its hope.

A glorious picture that! Christianity pure and simple that, and nothing more—that, and nothing less. It was for this that Jesus prayed. Will any hand be lifted to stay the day of the answer to His prayer?

The spiritual oneness of His people burdened His last days on earth—not even the agony of the Cross obscured His vision of a unified church. Oneness in harmony is the great thought of Christ for His people. He stands in their midst and prays for their oneness in the faith.

It is said that a German musician, though unable to speak English, had a highly cultivated ear—exquisitely sensitive to harmony, while discord would make him miserable. Passing down the street of one of our American cities, he heard music in a nearby church. Hoping to be inspired and helped he went in, but he found the music execrable, so far as its harmony was concerned. At first every singer seemed to be making discord. The impulse to retire seized him, but courtesy forbade such rudeness. He bravely endured the pain. Soon he discovered among the singers a trained voice—it was that of a woman. Though surrounded by discord she showed no sign of displeasure—she simply gave herself to the task of maintaining harmony in the midst of much discord.

The musician was charmed. The discord seemed to add to the power of her rich voice. Soon he observed that there was much less discord, and soon there was none; for one true sweet voice had swayed discord and converted it into harmony. Here is an illustration of the Genius of the Christian Movement under the leadership of the Holy Spirit.

To the spectator, the church has often seemed to be a great discordant mass, filled with strife and conflict. But the careful observer has discovered ONE in the midst of her who is maintaining harmony. He is dispelling discord —H^ is swaying the multitude, and bringing them into harmony with heaven. He is leading the symphony of God, and He is expecting His people to learn to sing with Him. He waits patiently for harmony, but in the world of strife and conflict He keeps up the music of salvation.

The Genius of the Christian Movement puts us on vantage ground as members of the great chorus. We have not

reached perfect harmony—far from it, but we are in position to follow His leadership with the *whole* company of the redeemed, till He shall have put away all discord, having transformed the universe into Heaven's own harmony, producing at last the divine ideal of the church—the grandest music of the ages. This prayer will sweep away all misunderstanding, all bitterness and all rivalry, when Heaven will come to earth and the Lord's people will be one forever. Let us come nearer, and yet nearer—let us fall at His feet till we learn to sing, with Him the glorious anthem of praise for a unified spiritual church on earth—a prototype of the Church Triumphant.

FELLOWSHIP IN JOURNALISM
BY REV. J.J. SUMMERBELL, D.D.[1]

Nineteen hundred years ago a reporter from heaven brought good news to some shepherds keeping watch over their flocks by night: "good news of great joy." The reporter came from a place of fellowship. He had good news for "all the people."

Many people are afraid of reporters. So, it was in this case. The history reads, "And they were sore afraid. And the angel said unto them, be not afraid; for, behold, I bring you good news of great joy which shall be to all the people: for there is born to you this day in the city of David a Savior, who is Christ the Lord."

The reporter then told them how they should know the child. The news was so interesting, that a multitude of reporters from the world of glory came in glory to the interview with the shepherds, saying, "Glory to God in the highest, on earth peace." They all brought good news of fellowship, the fellowship of heaven.

The essence of journalism, according to the sense of this Portsmouth meeting, is not the issuing of a literary production every day, whatever may be the etymology of the word. The chief thing that makes journalism of value is *news,* tidings. And that night, 1900 years ago, angels brought glad tidings to earth, the best ever reported: — "on earth peace."

The spirit of bearing glad tidings, good news, was imparted 1900 years ago so effectually, that the pamphlet that tells the story to this day is called "The Gospel According to Luke;" that is, the good news according to Luke. And there are other productions

<hr>

[1] Delivered on Thursday afternoon, September 17th, in the Christian church. Dr. Summerbell was for twelve years editor of the *Herald of Gospel Liberty*, at Dayton, Ohio.

with which we are somewhat familiar: —the good news according to Matthew, and according to Mark, and according to John: reporters to whom an ungrateful world accorded privations and sufferings because of their reporting the good news.

But the good news of these humble reporters, of whom the world was not worthy, has been published far and wide; and we are under its influence, and are met today in the spirit left by those reporters of heaven and earth, and which has sunk into the hearts of mankind, from reading the news they transmitted to us. And the spirit of their report of the birth, life, goodness, doctrine and death of Jesus Christ, is the spirit of fellowship. And fellowship entered into the thought of early Christians so deeply that I find the following language in the dispatches of some of their reporters: —

> That which we have seen and heard declare we unto you also, that ye also may have fellowship with us; yea, and our fellowship is with the Father, and with his Son Jesus Christ: and these things we write, that our joy may be made full. (1 John 1: 3-4.)

> And they continued steadfastly in the apostles' teaching and in fellowship, and in the breaking of bread and the prayers. (Acts 2:42.)

> If we walk in the light, as he is in the light, we have fellowship one with another, and the blood of Jesus his Son cleanseth us from all sin. (1 John 1:7.)

> God is faithful, through whom ye were called into the fellowship of his Son Jesus Christ our Lord. (1 Cor. 1:9.)

> He hath granted unto us his precious and exceeding great promises; that through these ye may become partakers of a divine nature, having escaped from the corruption that is in the world by lust. (2 Peter 1:4.)

"Partakers of a divine nature"! Think of that for one moment. Peter was the reporter who had the conception.

But some one here may object, that that was in ancient times; that the spirit of fellowship animating those early Christians, who had "all things common," has departed from the world; and those sectarian antipathies have now poisoned the breath of fellowship;

so that the religious journals of *our* time report hatred and strife, rather than communion and fellowship.

But such objection would be partly erroneous. There are probably no men of modern times in official station, that manifest a broader spirit of fellowship than the editors of religious journals. I say this from personal observation and experience. Let me explain:

—

For six or seven years I was associated in the paid editorship of different monthly religious magazines; and during that time not an unkind word as to my writing, as far as I know, was said in any cotemporary, though my articles were often on controverted subjects. Later, I was twelve years editor of the *Herald of Gospel Liberty*; and in the twelve years not a critical word was written in any religious exchange outside of my own denomination, that I know of, except one.

In that case I would not have known that my writing was referred to had I not received in an envelope addressed to "Mr. J.J. Summerbell" a clipping cut from the opposing paper and pasted on its letter-head. From this I inferred that the disagreeable clipping referred to my writing. Immediately I wrote to the editor of the supposed critical paper, suggesting to him in the best English then at my command that his action was not journalistic; that he should have made the matter plain in his paper, and not have called to his help a private envelope. Apparently by return mail I received a courteous letter from him, beginning with some such sentence as this: — "It looks like it; but I didn't do it." And he explained that he had been absent from his office when the objectionable act was done. And I think he was sincere. For, a number of years afterward, after I had delivered an appointed speech to a congregation numbering thousands of his denomination, informing them in my usual style that I was not in favor of their doctrines (or matter to that effect), while I was sitting in the hotel dining-room, he came over from his table to mine, stooped over me and said in a most pleasant manner, "You have the faculty of Gladstone; making a dry, parliamentary subject as interesting as a novel". ... Of course, his compliment was flattery, but it did not spring from a hateful heart, but from a spirit of fellowship. For I had often pounded his doctrine to the best of my ability.

And that spirit of fellowship I found to be characteristic of the *general body* of religious editors. If any of you remember my service, you may possibly recall that every week for years on the first page of my paper I was in the habit of quoting from other periodicals, making criticisms, opposing their statements sometimes, sometimes approving them, quoting for my own purposes and according to the line of thought I wished to impress; and yet in the whole twelve years, however much I may have deserved it, though the *Herald* was often quoted, I was never once accused of misquoting or garbling a passage, or construing it contrary to the meaning of the writer, or even unjustly, unless it was in the one case I have stated to you. I am not so foolish as to suppose that I never merited criticism.

Such charity among exchanges of other denominations could have come only from genuine fellowship; the true thing. Different religious papers said kind things of me on my leaving the editorial chair. The following is a sample: —

> Brother Summerbell is probably not aware that his courteous manner of treating his editorial brethren of all faiths and his large-heartedness have won for him a warm place in their hearts.

"Large-heartedness"! And yet I thought I had been acting like a sectarian! "After the most straitest sect of our religion I had lived a" . . . Christian. But these so- called sectarian editors, out of their own warm hearts, attributed good to me.

One cause of this broad spirit of fellowship among religious editors is the purity of the underlying principles which animate them in their calling. Nearly all of them being ministers of the gospel, they began their life work under the sense of moral obligation, feeling "called of God." In entering the editorship, it was with this sense continued. Therefore, in doing their work, they look at subjects from the standpoint of righteousness. They are men of God. I discovered that they were almost unfailingly on the right side on moral questions. Whether controversially, homiletically, or journalistically writing on any subject, they advocated righteousness, and condemned sin. And they were specific in this. They were not merely priests ministering at an altar, perfunctorily pronouncing age-worn formulas, but messengers of God, heaven's reporters, announcing to priests and laymen alike the principles of Paradise.

Thus, arrayed in one body on the side of heaven, in its great warfare against hell, religious editors, if honest men, logically warm toward each other, and gain a sweet spirit of fellowship. Remember how it was in ancient times. The heathen said, "See bow these Christians love one another." It was because the Christians of that day were engaged in common in a war against iniquity. They were the servants of the Father of love: in fact, they were his children, all in the family of the most affectionate Being of the universe; in the family of him who gave his only begotten Son that whosoever believeth in him should not perish; he so loved the world. This great war against sin and evil is caused by love. It is love that God uses to win sinners into the family: and it is a right instinct in them, developing into love, which moves the hearts of sinners to accept the love of God.

Modern religious editors are the heirs of the ancient Christians. Although a man may begin as editor with comparatively little love for fellow editors, the necessities of the great campaign draw him into a genuine fellowship with them. They have the same sufferings and triumphs; the same hopes and fears; the same loves and hates. When God is victorious in some skirmish, they write similarly exultant editorials. When sinners seem to prevail, their columns have a common pessimistic tone. They are brothers to each other in their happiness or misery.

I must not be understood to claim that *all* religious editors have a sweet spirit all the time. There are exceptions. I hold in my hand one editorial containing the following expressions of rhetoric, ... or animosity, toward another journal's editorial:—

"A whole bundle of misstatements ;"
"False Inferences;"
"Conspicuous example of inaccuracy
"Generally characteristic;"
"Misrepresented remarks;"

"Imaginary and false reports "Blunder;""

"False conclusions;"

"Other inaccuracies;"

"Misleading statements;"

"Most unreliable;"

"Totally Inadequate;"

"Distorted and garbled;"

"Sensationalism for revenue only."

The following are some more flowers that this same editor, in an editorial entitled "An Unchristian Spirit," lays on the table of another religious editor: —

This saintly personage raised a great to-do about the terms we employ. . .. That he has no objection to the use of strong terms is evident in the language he employs himself. For instance, "language of extreme coarseness, rampant recklessness, and savage brutality." Pretty fair for a writer who has nothing but "papa, prune and prism" for the monumental iniquities Of the Standard Oil system. It will doubtless be a great comfort to this pink of perfection to know that we have already apologized to the vampire and the bloodsucker for the unsavory association in which we placed them.

This editor had received the following compliment from another religious editor: —

The editor of the -----, of -----, in a recent editorial concerning Mr. Rockefeller, indulges in language of extreme coarseness, rampant recklessness and savage brutality. No editor of a reputable secular newspaper would employ such language. . .. What a Christian lover of his fellowmen that editor is! etc.

But such bouquets are rarely found in the religious editorial sanctums. They are not characteristic of the profession.

Righteousness is at the basis of their calling. They have not entered on their work for the earthly advantages of it. They do not write for wages, even though they receive salaries. They do their work as conscientiously as pastors of churches; and the exceptions are few. In my twelve years' service I only discovered two dishonest religious newspapers. Very few of them advocate what they do not believe. If they are not in harmony with some denominational doctrine, they usually leave it untouched. They try not to teach error. And their fellowship is genuine fraternity, based on character, on sonship to God.

It need not be supposed that this fraternity is merely a goody-goody communion of men who are superficial, or intellectually weak. They compare favorably with editors of great metropolitan dailies. While I was editor, a number of years ago, the following headlines and telegram appeared in the great dailies: —

DEFIES THE ALMIGHTY AND IS STRICKEN DEAD

ATHEIST CRIED ANATHEMA AGAINST GOD AND DIES INSTANTLY

Baltimore, Md., August 16. —Consternation reigns in the little town of Allen, in southern Maryland, over the strange death of Walter E. Whitney, a pronounced Atheist, but one of the most popular residents of the place.

On Sunday night Whitney was conversing with some friends when he suddenly exclaimed: —

"I defy the Almighty to strike me dead."

Instantly Whitney fell to the floor and when those about him picked him up he was dead.

Observing the effort made by one secular journal to account for the event on some basis beside that of a judgment of God, it struck me that it was important to learn if the telegram was true. Therefore, I sent the following letter: —

Dayton, Ohio, August 19, 1904.

Postmaster, Allen, Md.,

Dear Sir: —I have observed a telegraphic dispatch in the daily papers to the effect that a certain W.E. Whitney on Sunday night, August 14th, said: "I defy the Almighty to strike me dead;" and immediately fell and was taken up dead.

Will you kindly take the trouble to inform me if there is truth in the account?

Respectfully,
J.J. Summerbell.

To this letter I received the following reply: —

Allen, Md., August 22, 1904.
J.J. Summerbell, Dayton, Ohio,
Dear Sir: —It is all a mistake about Mr. Whitney. There is not at present and never was a man in our town by that name.

The writer from here has been on a "booze" for several days, so is liable to write most anything.

Very respectfully,
S.F. Malone, P.M., Allen, Md.

Then I watched my exchanges on this subject, and observed that the religious editors were not deceived: some of them made investigation and denounced the false telegram. Others treated it with silent contempt, instinctively detecting the fraud. They manifested capacity for discriminating as to history and weighing evidence. Some secular editors, however, wrote learned editorials, showing how the death of Whitney should not be attributed to divine judgment; but might be accounted for on psychological or physiological grounds. The religious editors first investigated, to learn whether the story was true.

And why should not this be so? The religious editors are *deeply* engaged in those subjects that are the greatest offered to human mentality: —God, immortality, righteousness, the human soul, philanthropy, social betterment, sectarian theology, missionary enterprise, heaven and other topics that expand and strengthen the Intellect.

All this may be said without detracting in the least from the praise due to the editors of our daily newspapers, who, as a class of men, are so great that the presidents of the United States for many years have with the approval of all Americans chosen many of them for our ambassadors to foreign nations. Probably at the present time some of our ministers to foreign courts are editors of

149

American dallies. It is with such men that I compare the editors of our religious journals.

Then it is not necessary to attribute the fraternal fellowship among religious editors to intellectual weakness. It comes from exalted character and mental ability, combined with their official relation to important events and great subjects.

The effect of this fraternity and fellowship among religious journalists is various: —

It tends, with some of them, to annul sectarian lines. The editors gain power to recognize the force of the arguments of other denominations. The editor learns more and more that there are not only sensible men, but delightful Christians, in all sects. He reasons, that if the editor of the journal, whose Christian spirit he so admires, is the product of the sectarian theology he has been in the habit of opposing, surely it is possible that there may be some underlying truth in that apparently reprehensible doctrine. Then he becomes more reserved in exposing its errors.

Fortunate is he, then, if he does not swing over to the other extreme, and lose his recognition of the importance of the differences between the doctrines of various sects. If he can preserve his deep reverence for truth, for truth in its great divisions, and for truth in its minute shadings, he has the possibility of becoming much like Jesus. He becomes a safe guide for the people: recognizing truth whenever presented.

Being thus able to see the force of the argument of an opposing sectarian, he is able wisely and effectually to refute the error that weighs the truth down and makes it ineffective or noxious. Not biased by partisan bigotry, he unconsciously labors to present the truth and to refute error in such a way that good may be the result. Like Jesus, intensely desirous to "bear witness to the truth," and to set religionists right, the religious editor who has profited suitably by his advantages of service and observation, will write with great force; but often in a way that will produce no reply, because of two reasons: — (1) The great power of the argument; (2) The kind spirit in which that argument is presented, which in itself makes the opposing editor who is inclined to reply seem to himself to be precipitating controversy.

There is another effect of this fellowship in journalism. It is not so blessed as that which I have discussed. Overcome by the fellowship of the editors of other sects, some editors seem to lose the power of independent thinking. They also cease to protect the interests they are in position to serve. Their journals become colorless, except in one feature. The paper "puffs" everybody mentioned in its editorial columns; too often spreading eulogy all over persons who are entire strangers to the editor. The editor smiles in every direction; horizontally and vertically. The editor even ceases to denounce sin, unless in such a way that no subscriber will take offense. The editorials of these journals might well be prepared by some literary hack, who might write for them all the common "original" matter. I have tried to imagine appropriate names for such papers; such as, The Inoffensive Outlook, The Friendly Advocate, The Applauding Spouter, The Weekly Sycophant, The Gospel Compliment, The Commending Recorder, The Model Eulogizer, The Sunny Sanctum, The Herald of Puffery, The Universal Flatterer, The Religious Toady, The Fawning Christian, The Obsequious Messenger, and the Subservient Humbug. But I have not yet suggested to any editor involved, an appropriate name that I thought he would adopt.

Such a spirit in an editor is a perversion of the holy and beautiful feeling of fellowship. If Jesus had been animated by it, he would have praised the long prayers of the Pharisees on the street corners: he would have directed the people to reverence the great learning of the scribes who sat in Moses' seat: he would have taught the Jews that the skeptical Sadducees undoubtedly had made important contributions to Scripture study, although not one of them ever gave anything worth telling to humanity; he would have called Judas a Napoleon of finance, and would have excused his deal with the chief priests as a necessary act of business, if Judas had ever been reported to him as having negotiated that celebrated bargain. . . . But Judas could never have sold such a Jesus: for nobody would have bought him. Jesus would have lived and died a common-place rabbi; or, even if he had attained to a place in the Sanhedrin, he would long ago have been forgotten.

But I am thankful that the spirit of fellowship in journalism produces few editors of this type. It usually makes them stronger, broader, and more faithful to the highest interests.

Finally, the chief and most beneficent effect of fellowship in journalism is that oneness of the general followers of Christ for which be so earnestly prayed. This oneness is steadily growing, even though tri-church unions and other sectarian combinations properly fail. The common people of the denominations, breathing in the truthful spirit of their editors, learning more and more of truth, become free. Every thinker knows that he who is both the master and slave of truth has greatest freedom. Jesus said, "The truth shall make you free." This freedom in its turn leads to truth, and truth leads to oneness. They who believe alike are likely to feel alike. And they who feel alike, are likely to love each other; to be drawn together. The denomination which has at its command the thought of a writer who has been constructively appreciative of the thoughts of the great writers of other bodies from week to week, as well as the great builders of the generations, will be certain to broaden its fellowship more and more through the years toward the oneness that Jesus desired: a oneness that does not depend on the unanimous reports of well packed committees; nor on the majority votes of denominational parliaments; nor on cheering for "the space of two hours, Great is Diana of the Ephesians;" nor on singing the long meter doxology for the rest of the afternoon ; . . . but on the freedom of the people who naturally love one another.

Fellowship in journalism will result in the purification of the doctrines of the church at large, in the purification of the morals of the general membership, and even in the purification of the worship of the sanctuary: —all which tend to unity.

Fellowship in journalism will finally lead to a beautiful unity even of the *denominations* of Christians. Their members will all be one, as the Father and the Son are one. Thus, the church will be lovely, symmetrical in her proportions, an honor to her Master, arrayed like a bride adorned for her husband in white raiment, which is the righteousness of the saints. And the world will then know that there is one Lord, one church, one hope, one God and Father of all, and one heavenly home. And there the journalists who here have fraternized with each other and been so promotive of final unity, will, no doubt, have the privilege of examining the great journal of that greater Editor, the "Lamb's book of life." And with what delight they will read the headlines and peruse the records written by the heavenly Editor, who died for them, no tongue can tell. But from that time on, for ever and forevermore, they will go in and out in full fellowship, under the directions of the great Editor, in their turn doing work, and still doing work, and doing still better work, that shall conduce to the development of the children of God. "Let us love one another."

THE PRESS AND MISSIONS
BY REV. O.W. POWERS, D.D.[1]

The *Herald of Gospel Liberty* had for its first issue a missionary motto. The paper owed its existence to the same spiritual quickening that gave rise to the modern missionary movement. It is not unfitting, therefore, that this centennial review be closed with a brief word concerning the relation of the press to the great enterprise of world evangelization.

When, in the fullness of time, God was ready to speak to the world through His Son, the Word was not only made flesh, but a body was also prepared for the reception of the words of the message. It cannot be considered other than of providential ordering

that the Greek language, the most perfect instrument for the expression of thought possessed by man, should be the current literary speech of the age in which the Gospel was proclaimed, thus insuring the most accurate preservation of the original message, as well as its most effective dissemination. The art of multiplying literary productions, too, was by no means in its infancy. The processes were slow, but not unknown or unusual.

It is said that three methods have always been available for the missionary in imparting his message—preaching, the testimony of his life, and the written words which can be read after he has gone. So, the church has proclaimed her message, first by direct evangelization, then by exhibiting a Christian civilization, and finally by embodying the message in a Christian literature. All this was accomplished by the primitive church.

But after the first great advance, which resulted in at least the

---

[1] Delivered on Thursday afternoon, September 17th, in the Christian church. Dr. Powers is Home Mission Secretary for the American Christian Convention, Dayton, Ohio.

nominal conquest of the then known world by the cross, we find that the church entered upon a period of less strenuous activity in promulgating the Gospel message. She lost sight of her divine mission of gospel telling, and her leaders became empire builders, contending with kings for authority over men. A new quickening was needed, in which the church, recalled to herself, might remember her commission, and take up again the great work of proclaiming to a lost world the unsearchable riches of Christ the old world,' waking out of sleep, found the new learning and the new preaching, calling men to new possibilities of mind and heart, while at the same time the restless discoverers were pointing to new realms awaiting the proclamation of the Word of Life. Says Dean Milman:

> Just at this period the two great final reformers, the inventor of printing and the manufacturer of paper, had not only commenced, but perfected, at one time their harmonious inventions. Books became cheap, were multiplied with a rapidity which seemed like magic, and were accessible to thousands. . .. The preacher was sought not the less on account of the vast extension of his influence. His eloquent words were no longer limited by the walls of a church, or the power of the human voice; they were echoed, perpetuated, promulgated over a kingdom, over a continent. ... To many the Book became the preacher, the instructor. even the confessor. The conscience began to claim the privilege, the right, of giving absolution to itself.

It is curious to note the misgivings with which the great discovery which meant so much for the spiritual development of mankind was given to the world. It is related that Gutenberg had a dream, in which a spirit seemed to come to him and say:

> John Gutenberg, thou hast made thy name Immortal, but at what a price I Bethink thee, what thou art doing I The ungodly are many more than the good. Thy work will but multiply their blasphemies and lies. Thou hast uncovered the bottomless pit. Henceforth a swarm of seducing spirits shall come forth, like a brood of Abaddon, and make the earth a hell. With such words the dream spirit sought to terrify him;

but awaking, be reflected that the gifts of God, though perilous, are never bad; that to endow intelligence with such a faculty was to open fresh fields to wisdom and goodness, both alike divine. "So," said he, "I proceeded with my discovery."

If Gutenberg could have foreseen the extent to which his forebodings have been justified, it would almost seem that he would indeed have wrecked his engine ere it was finished. But great as has been the mischief made possible, the power of the press for good has been immensely greater. The church had the first opportunity, and although in many instances she failed to keep the lead, she has never been wholly distanced by the powers of evil in the use of this mighty agency. The first impression made was of a Psalm. The highest art of the printer was expended upon the Holy Scriptures. The service of religion and the church seem to have almost monopolized the press in the early days, and it has continued to be in large measure the helper of all good and noble causes.

But it was not until the beginning of the modern missionary era that the immense power of the press as an evangelizing agency has become apparent. Dr. H.O. Dwight declares that, "Experience in the mission field has rediscovered the power of the press." The modern missionary conquests would have been utterly impossible without this mighty force.

It is difficult to estimate the part of the press in stimulating interest in missions, and in inaugurating the great modern movements. In 1792, Carey published his great "Inquiry," from which dates the beginning of his wonderful impression upon the church. The next year the *Evangelical Magazine* was founded. In 1794, in that magazine was published an address by Rev. David Bogue, of Gosport, England, from which is traced the origin of the London Missionary Society. In the same year were published "Letters on Missions, addressed to the Protestant Ministers of British Churches," which is characterized as one of the most powerful appeals that has ever appeared on the subject.

The early files of the *Herald of Gospel Liberty* show numerous quotations from the missionary journals of that day. These tidings from afar, with the news of the progress of the Gospel in strange

156

and almost unheard-of lands, must have thrilled those who read with a new sense of the power of the Christian religion.

It is impossible to estimate the power and influence of the missionary press in holding up to the churches of the home lands their opportunity and duty, and in promoting the intelligence and spirituality necessary for the great task of modern evangelical Christianity. The Blue Book of Missions for 1907 contains the names of nearly two hundred missionary publications for the home field, and the list is evidently incomplete. They probably place between two and three hundred million pages of carefully prepared matter before their readers every year. Besides this, the entire religious press devotes a large amount of space to distinctly missionary topics. An enormous amount of other missionary matter, such as tracts, bulletins, reports, and an ever-increasing volume of missionary books, is constantly being used in the missionary education of the churches. The new impulse to missionary publication given by the Student Volunteer Movement and the Young People's Missionary Movement has added immensely to this output. With all this, the churches are not yet fully aroused; but the existence of this immense body of literature is an indication that the time of awakening is at hand.

When we turn to the mission field, we see the real significance of the press as a factor in world evangelization. When Carey and Thomas began their work in India, the way seemed hedged up on every side. It was a tremendous task to find a way into the heart and life of the teeming millions of that great land. With little opportunity for direct evangelization, Carey turned his attention to the one method by which he could be sure to make at some time a permanent impression. He began to translate the Scriptures, and page by page, as fast as the translation was completed, he printed the leaves which were to be for the healing of that mighty race. His press was a rude affair. The natives thought it was the Englishman's idol, and mistook his absorption in its handling for worship. The barren years in which he struggled against the active opposition of the English government in India, as well as the indifference and superstition of the natives, were not wasted years. In the beginnings of a Christian literature, he laid the foundations of Christian

Missions in India so deep and solid that they could never be shaken.

A similar story can be told of every great attack upon the stronghold of heathenism. The press has been the mighty ally, the indispensable helper, of the missionary. It is so powerful an agency in the spread of the Gospel that it is almost a question which is of the greater importance—the man, or the book. A new missionary arriving in Japan, and proposing to devote himself to literary work, provoked severe comment from zealous critics. His reply was, that with a people as intelligent as the Japanese, a black missionary was as good as a white one. The Eskimos of Blacklead Island in Cumberland Sound could appreciate the power of the press, when they had mastered the wonderful principle of communicating by means of written and printed language. Said they: "Letters are as good as men, for they, too, can speak."

The achievements of the printed page, entirely apart from any living teacher, have been most remarkable. Doctor Clough, of Nellore, tells of a band of robbers, which by some means became possessed of some Christian tracts. By reading these they became interested in Christianity, and soon twelve of their number presented themselves for baptism. Sir Bartle Frere relates that all the inhabitants of a remote village in Deccan abjured idolatry and caste, removed from their temples the idols which had been worshiped there time out of mind, and agreed to profess a form of Christianity which they had studied out for themselves from a careful reading of a single Gospel and some tracts which had been left with them by accident. A merchant, who so far as was known, had never spoken of Christianity, and whose very name had been forgotten, had given these books, with some old clothing and other cast-off material to his servant. But his unconscious act had. planted the religion for which he cared nothing in the lives of a whole village full. Dr. John W. Butler states that the work of evangelical missions in Mexico began with the colporteurs who followed the American army with the Bible in 1847 and 1848. The Book has gone ahead of the missionary and prepared the way. He gives one instance of the conversion of a man and his wife from the reading of a single tract, and the formation of five Christian congregations through their influence.

In the evangelization of a literary people, the Christian press is indispensable. The influence of the native heathen or unevangelical literature must be counteracted. India is to become a nation of readers. Public libraries are being established. Periodicals and books are appearing from the native press in immense numbers. The most powerful literary productions of the Western world are being translated and circulated, and they are often of the most pronounced anti-Christian character. New classes are coming into possession of the keys of knowledge. Not so long-ago men were asking in India: "Can you teach a donkey or a horse to read? If so, you may possibly teach a woman." Now, it is estimated that over one million women of India can read. If Gutenberg's dream is not to prove true for these newly awakened minds, the mission press must redouble its efforts, not only to awaken new minds, but to supply those already awakened with proper mental food.

The same thing is true of other nations. Japan has a vigorous and powerful native press, and every kind of literature from Europe and America is finding circulation there. China is a literary nation, and her cry for Bibles and Christian literature is taxing the mission press to the utmost. The heart-breaking fact is that the missionaries cannot supply the needs of these people. Some one observing their anxiety in the face of the Insistent demand, proposes that an organization to help supply this demand might be called a "Society for the Prevention of Cruelty to Missionaries."

The indirect influence of the Christian press upon the native press is not to be overlooked. The presence of a vigorous and pure Christian periodical literature cannot fail to profoundly influence all other publications in the country where it circulates.

The most remarkable demonstration of the power of the press, however, is its influence in creating a new civilization among barbarous and savage races. The translation of the Bible into between four and five hundred languages and dialects, means that hundreds of races have been given the opportunity of participating in the best opportunities for education and development that the world possesses. Not only so, but the power of the missionary is increased many hundredfold. The native convert, by means of the book placed in his hand, can become a teacher. In Uganda, to become a Christian and a reader are synonymous terms.

Statistics give but a vague idea of the immense activity and importance of the mission press. Each year there are circulated in heathen countries two million, five hundred thousand Bibles and portions. The various tract societies put out fourteen million, five hundred thousand copies of their publications yearly. The mission publishing houses circulate annually besides, ten million, five hundred thousand copies. Three hundred and sixty-six periodicals are published in the mission fields, with an annual average circulation of nearly three hundred thousand copies.

The great work is but just begun. The church must make increasing use of this mighty force, both at home and abroad. "The great missionary weapon of the Twentieth Century must be a literature, saturated with the Gospel and efficient in the proclamation of the Christ."

HUNDRED YEARS OF RELIGIOUS JOURNALISM
BY REV. J.O. ATKINSON, D.D.[1]

One hundred years ago, *i.e.,* September 1, 1808, the first religious newspaper was issued, by Elias Smith, from a press in Portsmouth, New Hampshire. Our own Christian denomination, as is now well known and established, fathered that enterprise. And the paper Elias Smith issued is still being published as our own general church organ under the title, with which all of you are well acquainted, *The Herald of Gospel Liberty;* thus, making our *Herald* the oldest religious newspaper in the world.

At that time there were newspapers in plenty, but prior to that

time it was not thought that the religious idea was sufficiently interesting and popular to give a man enough to write about each week, and enough subscribers to support him in what he did write. I mean by this that religion and religious ideas, were not sufficiently popular to make weekly discussions worthy of interest and support. For, remember, at this time Thomas Jefferson, the third in succession to fill that office, was President of the United States; that even then a tide of French atheism was sweeping our land and country and that young men, in the old field schools, had as one of their queries in debate on Friday nights, "Resolved that there is no God." Remember, that this was four years before Adoniram Judson and his four associates were sent out as pioneer missionaries to India, and were ordered to return on the same *ship by which they* reached their des-

---

[1] Doctor Atkinson was invited to take part in the celebration or the *Centennial of Religious Journalism,* but being unable to he present, he prepared this address. Doctor Atkinson is editor of the *Christian Sun,* Elon College, N.C.

tination (1812). Remember, *that the doors* of China and Japan were closed then to missionaries. Remember, that prior to that time there was not a collegiate institution for women in all our land, and that in this very year Mrs. Emma Willard opened a school for young women at Middleburg, Vt., out of which grew, many years later, Mount Holyoke at South Hadley, Mass. (1837). Remember, that independent, or state colleges and universities were doing the work of higher education, and that the church college, as such, had not then come into existence. Remember, will you, that there were no railroads, no steamships, and consequently very poor mailing and postal facilities. That was a hundred years ago, when the religious newspaper was born.

This, of our *Herald of Gospel Liberty,* was a small beginning, it was a modest and unpretentious sheet. It came to herald a truth, and as the eternal years belong to truth, it began its career, not under impulse, nor with the blast of trumpets, but modestly, quietly, industriously, unassumingly. So, of all great world movements. They come un- honored, unsung, without noise and with little pretensions. The world itself, and light, and life, and order, grew out of a word calmly and quietly spoken— "Let there be light and there was light." The heavenly choir sang of the Redeemer's advent 'tis true, but the governor of the province, nay, not even the guard of the town, knew where the Christ was born. Small beginning that, without trumpets, without tumult, without triumphal train. Our American Independence was born, not amid the smoke of muskets at Lexington, not on the blood-stained field at Concord, nor at Valley Forge, nor yet at Yorktown, but by the quiet firesides of patriots' homes and peasants' cottages.

All great world events, issues, epochs and movements had small beginnings, modest advent, humble origin. So likewise, this of the religious journal. Now after the brief expanse of one hundred years, what? I shall not be able to tell you in these thirty minutes, but by brief comparisons some poor idea may be had. A hundred years ago one religious' newspaper with some few score readers. How stands the matter now?

In 1907 there were in the United States alone, 796 religious periodicals. The combined circulation of these last year was

15,269,067. Of these 796 distinct periodicals, two had a circulation each of 500,000. Six had a circulation each of 400,000; eight had a circulation each of 250,000; seventeen had a circulation each of 200,000; thirty-seven had a circulation each of 100,000; forty-five had a circulation each of 50,000; one hundred and thirty-seven had a circulation each of 20,000.

It is usual to multiply the number of subscribers by five to get the number of readers. This, however, would not be safe in esti- mating readers of religious papers, since several are taken by sin- gle subscribers. It is safe to measure by two and a half. Doing this we have between 35,000,000 and 40,000,000 people, one half of our entire population, touched and influenced by religious periodi- cals.

Counting these by mere numbers, how is this for a world movement, a truly great matter of humble origin and small begin- ning? One hundred years only a few score touched by our one sin- gle religious paper; today when the population has multiplied, compounded, and multiplied many times over again, one half of all this multitude touched each week by some of the 796 religious pe- riodicals.

But these figures only tell the smaller side, the physical, the mechanical, of a hundred years of religious journalism. May I in- vite you to larger considerations of the religious newspaper and what it has done, and helped to do, in these hundred years? I told you a while ago that higher education a hundred years ago was en- trusted almost, if not entirely, to private, independent, and state in- stitutions. There are today 450 higher institutions of learning in the United States. Of this number 5/9, or 250, are under the control of some branch of the Christian Church; while 4/9, or 200. are state, or independent, institutions. Now the great majority of students in these schools come from Christian homes. These 250 Christian in- stitutions are in many instances largely endowed, or supported by the contributions and gifts of Christian people. The religious news- paper, in most instances, made these institutions possible, sounded the bugle blast that called them to life and to activity, and in almost every instance brought their endowment into being.

The religious newspaper has always been the voice crying in

the wilderness; "Make straight the path to higher, and to Christian education." Take away from our church colleges, and religious institutions, the part that the religious paper has played, and a large part of their glory is gone. I can best illustrate this idea by reference to our own history, that as touching our own Elon College and our church paper, *The Christian Sun.* I can refer to this with boldness and without apology, for then I had no part in it all.

If you will refer to the columns of *The Christian Sun* from 1885 to 1890 you will see where the idea of our church college was fought out, won its splendid victory, and came into happy existence. By reference to these columns, writ out in courageous manhood, and given to the world in a boldness of a righteous cause, you will see that the Elon idea was not as popular then as now. Men doubted if our Christian cause and church could build, much less maintain, a denominational college. Some even doubted if we had the students to patronize it, much less the money to build it. Some said the idea was selfish and meager and MEAN. But what of your *Christian Sun* editor, and the faithful ones whose ideas and hopes he championed and nourished? If you care to know, come to the files in the *Christian Sun* office and they will tell you a story that you may not know, and of a heroic effort, and enterprise that you may have forgotten. (The brave, good man who wrote these burning editorials, stirring a lethargic and intellectually indifferent people to action and to an educational awakening is present in this conference and by the grace of God is with us today.)

The religious paper has always stood for the best and highest in educational pursuits, in moral and mental development. And the history of *The Christian Sun* as touching Elon College is the history in epitome of the religious newspaper as touching higher and Christian education. Take away from your church college the labor and effort of your church paper, and the glory and *success of the* former is unthinkable.

I have told you of only one of a whole category of causes and ideas the religious newspaper has stood for, made possible and developed in these hundred years of its honorable history and glorious record. I could fill out this half hour in telling of others no less obvious and no less potent. Almost every orphanage in all this broad land, (and thank God their number and usefulness are multiplying daily,) was championed first by some church or religious newspaper, and its idea forced home to fruition by the agitation, plea and persuasion of the editor and those who stood with him for this cause of Christian charity. (You cannot think of our Christian Orphanage without thinking of *The Christian Sun.*) When famine comes, earthquakes destroy, or fire and flood render thousands homeless, the voice of the religious editor is among the first to be heard for succor and relief.

Brethren, if I talk in these general terms, I fear you do not get the force and fact beneath and behind it all. I will, therefore, give you one concrete example; one instance of the usefulness and influence of a religious newspaper whose labor is personal, definite, specific, and whose usefulness is demonstrated even to the superficial mind, or even to the unthinking. . .. *The Christian Herald* of New York is one impressive illustration of the force of the religious paper in the field of human suffering. In fifteen years, this journal with the aid of a large number of readers, numbering over a million, has expended in various charities and benevolences, a grand total of over $3,750,000. For ten years it has maintained the Bowery Mission. Nearly every summer it feeds over an average of 30,000 waifs. In 1904, it sent $30,000 to the Macedonian sufferers; in 1906, $250,000 to the famine-stricken sufferers in Japan; in 1907, $50,000 to the famine sufferers in China. In the spring of 1908, the *Herald* increased the bread line of the Bowery Mission to 2,000 nightly.

The mention of this specific case is valuable, chiefly, as showing the spirit of the religious press, and as suggestive of the fact that, all throughout this great country, the religious newspaper is keeping the great national heart responsive to the cries of need and want and suffering.

And yet if I were to ask the name of the greatest and most powerful religious newspaper in New York, I should certainly not name *The Christian Herald.* Its work is on the surface. It reaps a harvest that others have sown. The New York *Christian Advocate, The Christian Observer,* and dozens of others, have labored and do labor to make possible the specific work of *The Christian Herald.* Who taught people to love and care for missions, so that the *Herald* could collect its thousands for mission purposes? It was the church organ. (A general religious paper versus church paper.) The church paper makes possible great ideas and higher spiritual notions.

But I weary you with detail. Examples multiply and so become commonplace and tedious.

The religious paper stands for the religious idea in the home, in the community, in the state. This is why it has achieved so marvelously since Elias Smith labored, in pain and in travail, till a great world movement was born. The deep of humanity's soul cried out to the deep of his great heart, and a world-idea was the answer to the cry, and the challenge. At the fountain of all our history, of all our achievement, of all our being is the religious idea and Elias Smith, a hundred years ago, dared to champion in the public arena, the call and cause of that idea. It was the German writer, Max Muller, who said:

> To my mind the great epochs in the world's history are marked not by the founding, nor by the destruction of empires; by migration of races, or by French Revolutions. The real history of man is the history of religion. That is the foundation that underlies all profane history; it is the light, the life, the soul of history; without it all history would be profane.

Max Muller was right, and the great Guizot is right when he declares "that all political and social questions refer for their ultimate solution, to the religious principle." It was as the bold champion of this basic principle, this fundamental of all ideas, that Elias Smith stands before us and challenges the admiration of men, the wonder of angels, and the plaudits of a religious race. When this is said, all is told. The religious idea is made prominent and the fundamental principle of civilization is laid bare and boldly championed. Why need I tell now of a hundred years of Christian missions, a hundred years of Christian philanthropy, of a hundred years of increasing fellowship and ever deepening brotherly love?

When religious journalism, with the sword of faith, struck the rock of God's eternal truth, these all leaped forth to make a new world and create a new race of men. I would have to trace each and all of these to tell the full story of a hundred years of religious journalism, for these came forth as the children, or co-laborers, of the idea of publicity of religious notions, conceptions and ambitions. I do not claim that the religious newspaper created these; I do not claim, for facts claim and history proves, that the religious newspaper was the forerunner of, and gave birth to, the idea that made these possible. Hear me then: Till the religious idea was brought into the broad light of day by discussion and publicity in the religious newspaper, you had no foreign missions. Until men dared fling their notions of world evangelization into the arena of public gaze and public discussion, through the medium of the religious newspaper, there was in the world no conception, and no plan of world evangelization. Until men dared champion in public print, of the religious newspaper, the idea of denominational schools, there were no church colleges. Any idea championed in public speech and print becomes more forceful, more fruitful.

I have another word. Somehow the idea has gone to a few, albeit, to the unthinking and to the unknowing, that the. religious newspaper has almost run its course; that before the modern immense and ever-increasing and all- devouring daily, the religious weekly is giving way and must ultimately go down. Unfaltering figures declare otherwise, and in this year of grace, 1908, the outlook for the religious newspaper is brighter than ever in all the past. Let us see. In 1900 there were 803 religious' newspapers. In 1907, there were only 796. In 1900, the

803 religious papers had a combined circulation of 11,717,-887; in 1907 the circulation was 15,269,067—a gain in circulation in seven years of 3,551,180, or an increase of over 30 per cent. — even greater than the increase in our ever rapidly increasing population.

In the state of North Carolina, the aggregate circulation of religious newspapers in 1900 was 48,810; in 1907 it was 69,741—an increase of over 40 per cent. And I need not go so far afield for figures. In these seven years our own *Christian Sun* has increased nearly 50 per cent, in circulation and our *Herald of Gospel Liberty* nearly 50 per cent.

There are about 35,000,000 church members in the United States. I have already shown that there are about 46,000, - 000 readers of religious newspapers. Thus, the field of the religious newspaper is a broad one, even taking in more in numbers than church members' family.

I sometimes approach a member of our church and ask him to take into his home, and the circle of his reading, his church paper. He replies, "I am already taking more papers than I read." He means by that his daily paper and his county paper. These carry him news of church and community and state! That man mistakes my motive, misinterprets my mission. I am asking him to take hold of an idea born of God, sent by heaven, championed by the bravest, and best of scholars and of men. Instead, he is contented with the "news." I am asking him to take bread for his and his family's soul; he tells me he is contented instead to see men in the world throw stones at each other. I am asking him to touch the fountain of God's deep; he tells me he is contented to hear the babel of men's lusts and passions and crimes. I ask him to turn aside now and then to read and think on things that prepare for eternity and God's future; he tells me he is absorbed now in the crimes of his age, the murders of his race and the blood of his fellowmen. Oh, my brother, I am seeking, God knows I am, to carry you a message of hope, and of cheer and of light and of life beyond the stars.

If you are a member of the Christian Church and do not take your own church paper, you may deem it a light and indifferent matter. God knows the motive that prompted Elias Smith to answer the call of a great world idea. He knows the motive, the hope, the ambition that have prompted all who have followed Elias Smith, to labor at the desk and toil at the pen and the press of the religious newspaper in these hundred years of its honorable history. That motive has always been, is today, to teach the noblest and the best in church and home and state.

MINUTES OF THE CENTENNIAL OF RELIGIOUS JOURNALISM

Under the auspices of the Christian Publishing Association, delegates, visitors and friends met at Portsmouth, New Hampshire, September 15th to 17th, 1908, to celebrate the One Hundredth Anniversary of the *Herald of Gospel Liberty*, the first religious newspaper ever published. Judge O.W. Whitelock, of Indiana, President of the Christian Publishing Association, presided as chairman, and Rev. Carlyle Summerbell, of Massachusetts, served as secretary. The committee on celebration, consisting of Judge O.W. Whitelock, chairman. Rev. T.S. Weeks. Rev. W.W. Stalev, D.D., Rev. A.H. Morrill, D.D., and Rev. D.B. Atkinson, A.M., had prepared a

program which was mostly carried out as arranged. Citizens from ten states and Canada represented the different portions of the brotherhood.

The first session was held Tuesday evening, September 15th in the Court Street Christian Church. Devotional Exercises were conducted by Rev. H.J. Rhodes. Addresses of welcome were made by Rev. F.H. Gardner, pastor of the Court Street Christian Church, Rev. Lucius H. Thayer, President of the Portsmouth Ministerial Association, His Honor, Mayor Hackett, of Ports mouth, and Rev. A.H. Morrill, D.D., President of the New England Christian Convention, on behalf of the respective interests with which they were connected. The singing of the Centennial Anthem composed by Rev. C.V. Strickland followed, after which a Response to Addresses of Welcome was given by Hon. O.W. Whitelock, President of the Christian Publishing Association. Benediction by the venerable C.P. Smith.

On Wednesday, September 16, at 9:00 a.m., the meeting convened in the Methodist church. Rev. L.B. Hess conducted the devotional exercises. Rev. F.H. Peters delivered an address, *"The Religious Press, the Exponent of Religious Freedom."* Mr. S.D. Gordon, representing the *Sunday School Times,* spoke on the *"Type Metal at Its Best."* Amos R. Wells, editor of the *Christian Endeavor World,* represented that paper and spoke upon *"Religious Journalism for Young People."* Rev. A.C. Youmans, A.B., B.D., spoke upon *"The Moral Influence of Religious Journalism."* Benediction by the venerable C.H. Roby.

The session of Wednesday afternoon was held in the Unitarian church, and Rev. H.W. McCrone had charge of the devotional service. An address by Rev. G.C. Waterman, representing *"The Morning Star,"* gave a history of *Free-Baptist Journalism.* Rev. Jos. S. Swaim, editor of *The Watchman,* spoke concerning *"The Development of Baptist Journalism."* A historical address, *"The Herald of Gospel Liberty"* was then delivered by Rev. D.B. Atkinson, A.M. Prof. J.N. Dales spoke upon, *"Other Denominational Publications."* Benediction by Rev. II.J. Rhodes.

On Wednesday evening the session was held in the Congregational church, and Rev. M.D. Wolfe conducted the devotional services. Rev. M. Summerbell, D.D., spoke upon *"The Educational Influence of Religious Journalism,"* and Rev. W.W. Staley, upon the *Principles and Progress of Religious Liberty."* Benediction by Rev. O.J. Hancock.

Thursday morning, September 17, the meeting convened in the Universalist church and the devotional services were conducted by Rev. Z. Knight. Rev. A.J. Northrup, representing *"Zion's Herald"* discussed *"Methodist Journalism" "The Christian Register"* was represented by Rev. Alfred Gooding, who gave a historical sketch of *Unitarian Journalism.* The Universalist fellowship was represented by Rev. Anson Titus who presented a historical discussion of religious journalism in that communion. A hymn by Rev. Edward Clark Hall, appropriate for the occasion, was sung by Rev. Harry J. Rhodes. An address, *The Genius of the Christian Movement"* was delivered by Rev. J. Pressley Barrett, editor of the *Herald of Gospel Liberty.* After this an informal discussion and conference was held in which the following brethren took part: Honsberger, Skinner, Gardner, Leighton, Hovey, Atkinson, Staley and Dales. Benediction.

In the Court Street Christian church, the last session of the celebration was held Thursday afternoon, the devotional services being in charge of Rev. H.A. Smith, A.M. Address, *"Fellowship in Journalism"* was delivered by Rev. J.J. Summerbell, D.D. The Convention Hymn composed by Rev. T.S. Weeks was sung by the congregation, led by Rev. A.H. Morrill, D.D.

Rev. O.W. Powers, D.D., then gave an address *"The Press and Missions"*

The following resolutions were presented by Rev. A.H. Morrill. I). D., and unanimously adopted.

WHEREAS, the Christian Publishing Association, through its trustees, have planned and carried out a celebration known as *"The* CENTENNIAL OF RELIGIOUS JOURNALISM" in Portsmouth, N.H., the city in which the *Herald of Gospel Liberty* was first issued, September 1, 1808, in the accomplishment of which there has been cheerful co-operation from various sources, therefore in order to express suitable appreciation of the same, be it

Resolved, that we, the delegates and attendants upon these services, return hearty thanks to the brethren of other denominations and publications for their presence, and the papers and addresses which they have given us, ministering so much to the success of this celebration.

Resolved, that our hearty expression of appreciation is due, and hereby cheerfully given to the pastors and friends of the Christian churches of Portsmouth, Rye and Kittery for their hospitality and assiduous efforts for our comfort and enjoyment during our attendance upon this Centennial.

Resolved, that our thanks are due and cheerfully extended to the pastors and officials of the Methodist Episcopal, Unitarian. Congregational and Universalist churches for their participation and interest in this celebration, manifested by their welcome to their church edifices for services in connection with this Centennial celebration.

Resolved, that we express our appreciation to the local and Associated Press for the reports of this gathering.

Resolved, that we thank His Honor, Wallace Hackett, Mayor of this city, for his presence and address of welcome at our opening service.

Resolved, that we express appreciation to the Boston and Maine Railroad for reduced rates to persons attending the Centennial.

The Chairman brought greetings from the Secretary of the Christian Publishing Association, Rev. Henry Crampton. Also, the Rev. Warren H. Denison, Secretary of the Mission Board of the Christian Church, sent regrets at not being permitted to attend the celebration and hopes for the continued success of the *Herald*. Kind expressions of like Import were also given on behalf of Rev. C.V. Strickland.

After singing the doxology, and benediction by Carlyle Summerbell, the Centennial came to a close with the fraternal spirit of true Christians abounding and the blessing of the Heavenly Father resting upon all.

O.W. WHITELOCK, Chairman.

CARLYLE SUMMERBELL. Secretary.

BIBLIOGRAPHY OF REV. ELIAS SMITH

Explanatory Note

A very large part of this bibliography has been compiled by Rev. Anson Titus, D.D., editor of the *Universalist Register,* Boston, Mass., who has kindly and with a scholar's instinct devoted much time to searching the libraries of Boston and neighboring cities, discovering much valuable matter in existence, not generally known, relative to the writings and publications of Rev. Elias Smith. Dr. Titus's efforts have been supplemented by the researches of others, who have been able to add considerable data, thus giving us a tolerably complete conspectus of the remarkable literary activity of Mr. Smith, and locating material upon which a future biographer may draw to give us a complete account of Mr. Smith's life and writings. Some of Dr. Titus's explanatory notes were enclosed in brackets; and all of the matter gathered by others has been so indicated.

The editor of this volume wishes to acknowledge his special debt to Dr. Titus, and to Rev. M.T. Morrill for special assistance, and his further obligations to those who have helped to make this bibliography adequate for practical purposes. There are doubtless many copies of Elias Smith's works in other libraries and private possession; and the editor hereby invites further contributions from any persons willing to give the same toward a *fuller* bibliography and list of places where material may be found.

Rev. Elias Smith's life and achievements concern more than the people of the Christian denomination, as he wrought a good part toward the religious freedom in which all denominations now share and rejoice. The New England newspapers chronicled his death, June 29, 1846, and spoke of him as "formerly a well- known preacher of several denominations."

List of Libraries

A.C.L.—Antioch College Library.
B.A.—Boston Atheneum.

B.P.L.—Boston Public Library.

C.L.—Congregational Library, Boston.

H.C.L.-—Harvard College Library.

T.C.L.—Tufts College Library.

U.H.L.—Universalist Historical Library.

N.E.H.G.S.—New England Historical and Genealogical Society, Boston.

R. Coll.—Roberts Collection, Christian Publishing Association, Dayton, O.

K.C.C.L.—Kansas Christian College Library.

C.P.A.—Christian Publishing Association.

LIST OF ELIAS SMITH'S WRITINGS

The Clergyman's Looking Glass. The main pillar of anti-Christ's kingdom shaken, and the folly of Jannes made manifest: being an examination of Mr. [--] Osgood's arguments in favor of the anti-Christian practice of sprinkling children, under pretense of baptizing them. Boston. Printed for the author, 1804. 36 pp., 12 mo. B.P.L.

No. 4. *Examination of D— Osgood on "Sprinkling."* Boston, 1804. No. 1. Second Edition, Portsmouth, 1803. B.A., H.C.L.

Five Letters with Remarks. Boston, 1804. pp. 36. C.L.

A Reply to "How Shall I Know that I am Born Again." Boston, 1804. pp. 36. B.A.

Daniel Humphreys, born 1740, died 1827, published a *"Letter to Elias Smith on his late performance entitled* A Reply to this Congregational-Methodistical question: Why can you not commune with us, seeing we are willing to commune with you?'" Portsmouth, printed by W. and D. Treadwell, 1804. pp. 23, 12 mo. B.P.L.

Letter to Daniel Humphreys, Sandemanian Teacher. Portsmouth, 1804. [Imperfect.] B.A. [Daniel Humphreys, Esq., was the son of Rev. Daniel Humphreys, Derby, Conn. He was of

Yale College, 1757. He was a schoolmaster in New York City, and at close of Revolutionary War removed to Portsmouth, N.H. He was a teacher of the little flock of Sandemanians in Portsmouth for a long series of years. He died Sept. 30, 1827, aged 87 years.]

The Light not Clear nor Dark. Discourse, Hopkinton, Sept. 5, 1804. Boston, 1805. B.A.

The Whole World Governed by a Jew: or the Government of the Second Adam, as King and Priest. Exeter, 1805. pp. 84. B.A. [Rev. J.F. Burnett, D.D., Dayton, O., has one copy in his library.]

Hymns, Original and Selected for the Use of Christians. 1805, Portland. [Abner Jones and Elias Smith.]

Smith and Jones' Hymn Book. Seventh Edition [1816], a small, neat pocket volume. $1.00. [First Edition 1805, Portland.]

The Doctrine of the Prince of Peace and His Servants. Concerning the end of the wicked, contrasted with the doctrines of the prince of this world, and his servants, upon the same subject; proving that the doctrines of the Universalists and Calvinists are not the doctrines of Jesus Christ and the apostles. Review of Samuel Shepherd. Printed at Boston. Sold by the author [etc.] in Portsmouth. 48 pp., 12 mo. 1805. B.P.L., B.A., H.C.L.

The Christian's Magazine, Reviewer and Religious Intelligencer: consisting of subjects Historical, Doctrinal, Experimental, Practical and Poetical. Portsmouth, 1805. Vol. 1: 1-5. C.L. [Vol. 1, No. 1. R. Coll.] [Vol. 1, No. 3, in the Library of Rev. J.F. Burnett, D.D., Dayton, O.]

The Man in the Smoke, and a Friend Endeavoring to Help Him Out, etc. Remarks on T. Baldwin's Sermon—The Purpose of God. 1805. pp. 36. B.A., C.L.

The Day of Judgment. A sermon, 1805.

Discourse on the Resurrection. 1806.

A *Letter to Mr. E.R. Sabin.* 1806.

*The Age of Enquiry, Christian's Pocket Companion and Daily As-
sistant:* Calculated also for the Benefit of the Rising Generation, in Leaving them the Truth. By Elias Smith. Him shall
ye hear in all things. —Peter. Train up a child in the way he
should go. --Solomon. Exeter, 1807. pp. 154. [R. Coll.]

A Sermon on New Testament Baptism. 1807.

Herald of Gospel Liberty. By Elias Smith. 1808-1817. Only a par-
tial set in Boston Public Library. Card Catalogue has this
comment, "Probably the first religious paper published in
America." [Practically complete file in H.C.L. 1808-1811,
three volumes in one, C.L. 1810-1813, four volumes in one.
R. Coll. 1808-1813, six volumes in one. C.F.A. 1808-1814,
seven volumes in one. K.C.C.L., A.C.L. Vol. 8, No. 2, and
Vol. 8, Aug., 1816-Oct., 1817, bound, in the Library of
Rev. J.F. Burnett, D.D., Dayton, O.

Three Sermons on Election, describing the Election of Christ; An-
gels; Patriarchs; Nation of Jews; Prophets; Apostles; Saints.
[Exeter, 1808, pp. 126. Small pocket volume.] B.P.L. [R.
Coll.] H.C.L.

*Sermons Containing an Illustration of the Prophecies to be Ac-
complished from the Present Time Until the New Heavens
and Earth are Created, when all the Prophecies will be
Fulfilled.* 1808. Exeter, 12 mo., pp. 300. U.H.S. [R. Coll., 3
copies.]

*The Loving Kindness of God, displayed in the Triumph of Republi-
canism in America,* being a discourse at Taunton [Mass.],
July 4th, 1809. pp. 36, 12 mo. B.P.L., B.A.

Discourse on Government and Religion. Gray, Me., July 4, 1810. Portland. 12 mo. B.A.

The History of Anti-Christ. Portland, Herald Printing Office, 1811. 120 pp. 24 mo. B.P.L.

New Testament Dictionary, containing the New Testament meaning of 108 words; pocket volume, $1.00.

A *New Testament Dictionary.* By Elias Smith. "Understandest thou what thou readest?" "How can I, except some man should guide me?"—ACTS. Philadelphia. Printed and sold by the author. 1812. [R. Coll. 2 copies.]

A *New Testament Dictionary.* Originally written by Elias Smith. Now revised with additions, etc., by Robert Foster. To which is added a *Brief History of Our Savior, and the Lives, Sufferings and Martyrdom of the Apostles,* etc. "Search the Scriptures." Portsmouth; *Christian Herald* office. 1832. [R. Coll.]

Philadelphia County Christian Church. Circular, account of the withdrawal of S[mith] from the Church. Philadelphia, 1813. B.A.

A Small Volume of Hymns just published, entitled, Songs of the Redeemed, for the Followers of the Lord. [Ante 1816.]

Volume of Sermons: Sermons in Pamphlets on various subjects, *etc., etc.* [Ante 1816.]

The Life, Conversion, preaching, Travels and Sufferings of Elias Smith, written by himself. And thou shalt remember all thy way which the Lord thy God led thee these forty years in the wilderness. —Deut. 8:2. Gather up the fragments that remain that nothing be lost. —John 6: 12. Vol. I, Portsmouth, N.H. Printed by Beck and Foster; sold by the author, No. 2 Ladd St., and James F. Shores, No. 1 Market

Street, and by Christian preachers in the United States and the book stalls. 1816. Quarto. 406 pp. N.E.H.G.S., T.C.L., U.H.S., B.P.L. two copies. [R. Coll., 2 copies, one the edition of 1840. Back fly leaves advertise vegetable medicines. Rev. J.J. Summerbell, D.D., Dayton, O., has a copy in his library, revised in 1840, and Mrs. Emily Parker, Woodstock, Vt., has a copy of the first edition.]

Edition of 1840, with portrait. H.C.L. [There are several pages additional to edition of 1816, mentioning that he resided in Boston from June, 1816; and his design to publish a second volume, containing autobiography from 1817 to date. He became once more a member of the Christian Church in Portsmouth, Feb. 20, 1840, and once more a minister in their fellowship. He resided for the most part, between 1840 and 1846, in Providence, at the home of a daughter. He died however in Lynn, June 29, 1846. — Anson Titus.]

Letters of J. Rand to [Elias] Smith. Examination of his thirteen reasons for believing the salvation of all men. Danville. 1818. B.A. [R. Coll.]

The Judgment of This World: The Prince of this World Cast Out: and all Men Drawn to Christ. 1819. 12 mo. pp. 13. U.H.L.

Herald of Life and Immortality. Vol. I.B.A. [This was a quarterly magazine and had eight issues from January, 1819, to October, 1820, making one volume, with an index. pp. 288. The Herald of Life advocated phases of religious doctrines accepted by many Universalists. Elias Smith maintained his own way and manner of advocacy of whatever doctrine he was at the time most interested in. He was an original man, unique in character and delighted in being in the public eye. In spite of his theological wanderings, he held to the Bible, as its own and best interpreter.]

A *Sermon on Nebuchadnezzar's Dream on the Image of Gold, Silver, Brass, Iron and Clay, and the Stone which Ground the*

Image to Powder. Delivered in Boston, May 4, 1820. 12 mo. pp. 40. T.C.L., B.A., C.L., B.P.L.

A *Collection of Hymns for the Use of Christians.* Elias Smith, compiler. Boston. Printed and sold by Manning and Loring. [180—] PP- 72. B.P.L.

Extract of a Letter from Elder Elias Smith to Elder Elijah Shaw, Jr., dated Boston, Nov. 15, 1826. Gospel Luminary, West Bloomfield, N.Y., Jan., 1827. R. Coll, and Library of Rev. J.F. Burnett, D.D., Dayton, O.

Sermon in the Morning Star and City Watchman. Vol. II, No. 6. 1829. B.A.

A *Brief Review of Two Numbers of Elder E. Smith's Periodical ("The Morning Star and City Watchman")* appears in *The Gospel Luminary,* West Bloomfield, N.Y., Aug., 1827. R. Coll. Library of Rev. J.F. Burnett, D.D., Dayton, O.

Letter from Elias Smith to Joseph Badger, editor of "The Christian Palladium," published at Union Mills, N.Y., in the issue of October 2, 1837, Vol. 6. No. 11, page 170. R. Coll.] The medical publications of Elias Smith are beyond our knowledge. There were many editions. Mr. Smith traveled much, lecturing upon his system of medicine, sold his books, and preached as many Sundays as he could, in whatever pulpit chanced to be vacant, or into which he was invited. He was well-known throughout his circuits. He had a controversy with Dr. Thomson, the founder of the medical system of which he was an enthusiastic promoter and physician.

The Medical Pocket Book. Boston. Bowen. 1822. 168 pp. 16 mo. Elias Smith, M.D. [Elias Smith was ever called Doctor, but whether he was an M.D. or where he obtained the degree, is not known to the writer.] B.P.L.

The Minutes and Report of a Council, convened for the purpose of

*inquiring into the merits of a pamphlet entitled, "A State-
ment of the Conduct of Elias Smith toward Dr. Samuel
Thomson."* Boston, printed by H. Bowen, 1822. pp. 12, 12
mo. B.P.L.

<u>*A*</u> *Narrative of the Life and Medical Discoveries of Samuel Thom-
son, M.D.,* [1769-1843] containing an account of his system
of practice, and the manner of curing diseases with vegetable medicine upon a plan entirely new. Second edition.
1825. B.P.L. [This book contains a chapter upon his relations with Elias Smith, concerning the system of their medical practice. It is the writer's mind that the discussion continued long, and each had his supporters. —A.T.]

The American Physician and Family Assistant. In five parts, containing: I. A General Description of Vegetable Medicines.
II. The Manner of Preparing them for Use. Description of
Diseases, and Manner of Curing them. A Description of
Mineral and Vegetable Poisons, given by those called Regular Doctors, under the Name of Medicines. Health Vari-
ously Illustrated. Boston, 1826. Third edition 1832. Fourth
edition 1837. H.C.L. [Third edition, R. Coll]

The People's Book: Address on poison, health, disease, vegetable
medicine and manner of curing the sick. Boston, 1836.
B.A.